Curriculum Focus

Famous journeys

John Davis

Hopscotch
A division of MA Education Ltd

Curriculum Focus series

History

Famous Events Key Stage 1
Famous People Key Stage 1
Toys Key Stage 1
The Tudors Key Stage 2
The Victorians Key Stage 2
The Invaders Key Stage 2

Geography

Islands and Seasides Key Stage 1
The Local Area Key Stage 1

Science

Ourselves Key Stage 1
Animals, Plants and Habitats: Key Stage 1
Materials: Key Stage 1

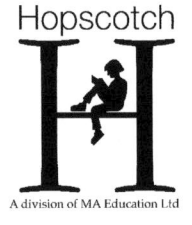

Hopscotch
A division of MA Education Ltd

Published by Hopscotch,
a division of MA Education,
St Jude's Church, Dulwich Road,
London, SE24 0PB
www.hopscotchbooks.com
020 7738 5454

© 2010 MA Education Ltd.

Written by John Davis
Designed and illustrated by Emma Turner
Front cover illustration by Yana Elkassova

ISBN 978 1 90539 082 3

All rights reserved. This book is sold subject to the condition that it shall not, by way of trade or otherwise, be lent, hired out or otherwise circulated without the publisher's prior consent in any form of binding or cover other than that in which it is published and without a similar condition, including this condition, being imposed upon the subsequent purchaser.

No part of this publication may be reproduced, stored in a retrieval system, or transmitted, in any form or by any means, electronic, mechanical, photocopying, recording or otherwise, without the prior permission of the publisher, except where photocopying for educational purposes within the school or other educational establishment that has purchased this book is expressly permitted in the text.

Every effort has been made to trace the owners of copyright of material in this book and the publisher apologises for any inadvertent omissions. Any persons claiming copyright for any material should contact the publisher who will be happy to pay the permission fees agreed between them and who will amend the information in this book on any subsequent reprint.

Contents

Introduction   7

Chapter One   Amelia Earhart   8

Chapter Two   Roald Amundsen   34

Chapter Three   Neil Armstrong   58

Chapter Four   Ellen MacArthur   84

Useful Resources   111

Introduction

One of the most important ways laid down for KS1 children to be introduced to history is through the study of famous people and their involvement in past events from the history of Britain and the wider world.

Such studies can help them learn the vocabulary of history, highlight the differences between then and now and teach them how we know what happened in the past. Furthermore it challenges them to think more closely about the questions people ask about events in the past and assists them to understand key historical concepts like chronology and change.

The purpose of this comprehensive resource-one of the *Curriculum Focus: History* series-is to incorporate all these elements and to inspire teachers, especially the non-specialist, to teach history with confidence.

The four journeys in this book involve the pioneering explorers and travellers Amelia Earhart, Roald Amundsen, Neil Armstrong and Ellen MacArthur. They have been specially selected to provide an international flavour and to cover the travel locations of air, land, space and sea. While history and geography feature strongly there are many cross-curricular elements associated with the themes and activities outlined including mathematics, literacy, science, design technology and information technology.

The book is intended to be flexible enough to integrate into any school's own scheme of work or to be dipped into as and when required.

- Each chapter contains detailed background information about the topic written at the teachers' level and resources providing stimulating pictures, diagrams and maps.

- This is followed by detailed lesson plans on the theme, each based on clear historical objectives. Resources are listed and starting points for the whole class are outlined. Lesson plans are organised with guidelines to provide essential information and assist with the teaching process.

- The group activities that follow are based on highly practical differentiated tasks at three ability levels that reinforce and develop the content of the lesson. Guidance is given about how children can be prepared for these activities and how they might be organised and supported.

- The main points of the lesson are revisited in plenary sessions that are wide ranging, interactive and sometimes include drama and role play.

- At the conclusion of each chapter there are ideas for support and extension and suggestions.

Chapter 1

Amelia Earhart

TEACHERS' NOTES

Early life

Amelia Earhart first saw an aeroplane at the age of ten when she visited the Des Moines State Fair near her home in Iowa in 1908. Her father tried to persuade her sister Muriel and her to take a flight. The girls flatly refused and Amelia is reported to have said when looking at the old biplane, 'It was a thing of rusty wire and wood and not at all interesting.'

How her views on early flying machines were to change, as later in life she became one of the world's most formidable aviators with a string of record-breaking long distance flights to her name and top international honours.

Amelia Earhart was born on July 24th, 1897 at the home of her grandfather, a former judge, who was a leading citizen in the town of Atchison, Kansas. Her parents moved several times when Amelia was young as her father, a lawyer, tried to find suitable work.

Amelia, known as Meeley or Millie, and sister Muriel, usually called Pidge, were adventuresome girls who spent long hours playing outside, hunting rats, keeping moths, butterflies and toads as pets and building large model toys including a miniature roller-coaster.

Throughout what was often a difficult and disrupted childhood, Amelia carefully considered her future career. She kept a scrapbook of newspaper cuttings about successful women in predominantly male-dominated fields including film direction, law, business management and mechanical engineering.

In 1914, Amelia's mother took the two girls to live with friends in Chicago where they were educated privately in preparation for going to college. Muriel later moved to Toronto in Canada where she came into contact with soldiers returning from the First World War battlefields in Europe. It was while visiting her that Amelia decided to train as a nurses' aid and she served with the Voluntary Air Detachment at a military hospital until the end of the First World War in 1918.

First flight

By 1919, Amelia, now twenty-two, had rejoined her parents who were living in California. Soon after her arrival, Amelia and her father went to an 'aerial meet' at Daugherty Field in Long Beach organised by Frank Hawks, a well known air racer. The following day, having been given a set of goggles and a helmet, she climbed aboard an open cockpit biplane and made a ten minute flight over the countryside around Los Angeles. 'As soon as we left the ground and got two or three hundred feet in the air, I knew I myself had to fly,' she said later.

Soon afterwards, Amelia met a local woman who gave her flying instruction and soon she was taking regular lessons with Anita 'Neta' Snook who flew a Curtiss JN-4 Canuck at Kinner Field, Long Beach. Within months Amelia had purchased her own Kinner Airster aeroplane, calling it The Canary because of its bright yellow colour. Planes were unreliable in those days and slow. There were several accidents at this time and Snook often had reservations about Amelia's skill as a pilot. In October 1922 Amelia set a world record for female pilots by taking the aircraft to 4300 metres (14000 feet). Early the following year she became the sixteenth woman to be issued with a pilot's licence worldwide.

By the autumn of 1925 Amelia had moved to Boston where she took employment as a social worker. She immediately became a member of the Boston Chapter of the Aeronautic Association and invested what little money she had in a company intending to open an airport and build Kinner aeroplanes in Boston. She took every opportunity possible to promote flying, especially for women, and was regularly featured on the pages of The Boston Globe newspaper which described her as 'one of the best women pilots in the United States.'

Life changes

It was a phone call on April 27th, 1926 that changed Amelia's life for forever. It came from Captain H.H. Railey and was unequivocal. 'How would you like to be the first woman to fly across the Atlantic Ocean?', he said. A New York publisher, George Putnam, had asked Railey to find a woman who was willing to make the flight. Within a week, Amelia had attended a meeting with Putnam in New York and plans were already being made for the venture although for the first Trans-Atlantic journey Amelia would only be a passenger.

Amelia had no experience of flying multi-engine machines or using instruments, so it was decided two men, Wilmer Stultz and Louis Gordon, would pilot the aircraft, a three-motor Fokker named The Friendship. Amelia would have the official title of 'commander of the flight.'

Several days were wasted waiting for the weather to clear but eventually on June 17th, 1928 the aircraft left Halifax, Nova Scotia in Canada. Bad weather, particularly dense fog, would again slow up the crossing of the Atlantic but finally the plan landed at Burry Port in South Wales, very low on fuel. The flight had taken just over twenty and a half hours. Commented Amelia, 'I was a passenger on the journey... just a passenger. Everything that was done to bring us across was done by Stultz and Gordon. Any praise I can give them they ought to have. I do not believe women lack the stamina to do a solo trip across the Atlantic but it would be a matter of learning the arts of flying by instruments only, an art which few men pilots know perfectly now.'

When the crew of three returned to the United States they were treated as top celebrities. There was a ticker tape parade through the streets of New York and the three fliers were guests of President Calvin Coolidge at the White House, Washington. George Putnam kept Amelia constantly in the spotlight. She went on lecture tours, wrote a book about the journey and became closely associated with a number of successful marketing campaigns, selling such things as travel luggage, women's clothing and sportswear.

Collecting records

In September 1928, Amelia made the first solo flight by a women across the United States of America from coast to coast. Air Races and altitude and distance record attempts in both aircraft and autogyros followed as well as lecture tours, article writing and countrywide visits. The following year she was appointed assistant to the general transport manager at Transcontinental Air Transport (later the airline company TWA) with the special responsibility of attracting women passengers. Soon she had broken several women's speed records in her Lockheed Vega aircraft. Then, after marrying George Putnam early in 1931, Amelia began to plan her lifelong ambition, a solo flight across the Atlantic. Several other women pilots had announced their intentions of attempting the crossing so the couple knew they would have to waste no time if they wanted to stay ahead of the field.

Going solo

Five years on, it would be the first solo flight across the Atlantic since the one made by the American aviator Charles Lindbergh. Amelia, however, was determined not to follow the same route and would fly instead from Newfoundland with the British Isles as her destination. On May 20th, 1932, Amelia's modified Lockheed Vega began its journey. Since she did not drink either tea or coffee she carried smelling salts with her in order to keep awake throughout the flight. She also prided herself on travelling light so the only other provisions she carried with her was a thermos flask of soup and a can of tomato juice. There were problems on the flight including failed instruments, a cracked exhaust pipe and icing on the wings but just short of fifteen hours after take-off, she landed in a field in Londonderry, Northern Ireland. Not only had she completed the longest non-stop flight by a woman but had covered the distance in the quickest time. Back in America she was awarded the Distinguished Flying Cross, the Gold Medal of the National Geographic Society and became friends with the President, Franklin Roosevelt and his wife. A number of other solo flights followed. These included Hawaii to California in 1935 in which Amelia became the first pilot of a civilian aeroplane to carry and use a two-way radio-telephone.

Global ambitions

Towards the end of 1935, Amelia began to formulate plans for her most ambitious project so far and she set the standards high. Not only would she be the first woman to fly around the world, she would circumnavigate the globe at its waist, close to the equator and the longest distance possible. A new aeroplane would be needed and for this project the Lockheed Electra 10E was selected. To assist her on the flight a top class navigator was named. He was Fred Noonan, a former navigator on the PanAmerican Pacific Clipper who got the job because of his familiarity with the expanses of ocean being flown over. The first attempt in March 1937 failed soon after it started. The aeroplane crashed while trying to take off from Luke Field, Pearl Harbour in Hawaii. There was no fire but the aircraft was badly damaged and was shipped back to the United States for urgent repairs.

Second attempt

While the Electra was being repaired Amelia and her husband worked hard to gather additional funds in preparation for the second attempt. This time, because of the prevailing winds and general weather conditions, it was decided to fly west rather than east. As she got ready for the flight Amelia announced, 'I have a feeling there is just one more good flight left in my system and I hope this trip is it. Anyway when I have finished this job, I mean to give up long-distance flying.' Amelia, with Fred Noonan navigating, left Florida on June 1st, 1937. They travelled first to San Juan on the island of Puerto Rico and from there skirted the north east edge of South America before crossing the Atlantic to Africa and from there on to the Red Sea. The next stage, to Karachi, now in Pakistan, was another first and then the pair flew on to Calcutta, Rangoon, Bangkok, Singapore and Bandung. Monsoon rains prevented them from leaving here for several days. Repairs were made to the long distance instruments that had been causing trouble and Amelia spent several days recovery from a bout of dysentery. It was on June 27th that the Electra was finally able to travel on to Port Darwin in Australia. Here the direction finder was again repaired and the parachutes removed from the aeroplane and packed ready for the journey home. Apparently they would be of no value over the Pacific Ocean. When the two fliers reached Lae, New Guinea on June 19th they had flown 35000km (22000 miles) and there remained 11000km (7000 miles) still to go, all over the Pacific. Amelia and Fred Noonan took off from Lae at midnight on July 2nd (00:00). The aircraft was loaded with some 1000 gallons of fuel, enough to permit about twenty hours of flying. At 08:00 Amelia made her last radio contact with Lae. She reported being uncertain of her course for Howland Island, the next stop, and being low on fuel. No-one heard from Amelia or Fred Noonan again.

Detailed search

When it became clear that the Lockheed Electra was missing an immediate search plan moved into action. The area immediately around Howland Island was scoured first and then the search was extended further afield. United States Navy warships were called to the scene and search aircraft flew low over uninhabited islands looking for signs of life. Official search efforts lasted for over a week. The Navy and Coast Guard co-ordinated search was reported to have cost some four million dollars, the most intensive and costly in the history of the United States up until that time.

Despite all the effort involved, no sign of Amelia, Fred Noonan and the Electra 10E was found. Immediately after the end of the official search, George Putnam financed a private search in the region lasting several months and including visits to nearby island groups. Back in the United States, Putnam became a trustee of the Amelia Earhart estate so he could pay for the searches and settle other bills. In order to manage the finances Putnam was granted permission to have a seven-year waiting period waived and as a result Amelia was officially declared dead on January 5th, 1939. In a letter sent to George Putnam during the course of the flight she had written, 'Please know that I am quite aware of the hazards. I want to do it because I want to do it. Women must try to do things as men have tried. When they fail, their failure must be but a challenge to others.'

Conflicting theories

Speculation about what happened to Amelia Earhart and the Lockheed Electra has been rife ever since the event happened. Many researchers believe the aircraft may have drifted off course and then just ran out of fuel forcing it to ditch into the sea just short of Howland Island. Lack of a definitive position and the depth of the water in this part of the Pacific Ocean make underwater searches difficult. Other island groups in the same region have also been thoroughly searched for remains especially by an organisation called The International Group for Historic Aircraft Recovery (TIGHAR) that launched its own Earhart Project in 1988. Small numbers of artefacts have been found on the then uninhabited Gardner Island (now called Nikumaroro) yet these too have proved inconclusive. Some theories put forward appear to be nothing more than fantasy. One suggested that Amelia disappeared while on a spying mission against the Japanese while another claimed that Earhart and Noonan had been captured and executed when the aircraft had crashed on the Japanese occupied island of Saipan. Even more far fetched was the story published in a book that Amelia had survived the flight, moved to New Jersey, changed her name and remarried. A full explanation will probably never be known. As one researcher wrote, 'The mystery is part of what keeps everyone interested. In part, we remember her because she's our favourite missing person.'

Amelia's legacy

Amelia Earhart became a worldwide international celebrity during her lifetime. Among her characteristics she displayed courage, coolness under pressure, persistence and determination. These strengths together with the circumstances of her disappearance have turned her into a feminist icon. Numerous articles and books have been written about her life and she is often cited as an inspirational role model.

Her accomplishments in flying inspired generations of female aviators especially the one thousand plus women pilots of the Women Airforce Service Pilots (WASP) who ferried military aircraft, towed gliders and served as transport pilots during the Second World War.

The house in which Amelia was born is now the Amelia Earhart Birthplace Museum and is maintained by the Ninety-Nines, an international group of women pilots of which Amelia was the first elected president.

In addition to many books, a number of films have been made about Amelia Earhart's life including Flight for Freedom (1943), Amelia Earhart (1976) and Amelia Earhart: The Final Flight (1994). The latest version called simply Amelia was released in cinemas late in 2009. Directed by Mira Nair, it stars Hilary Swank in the lead role and Richard Gere as George Putnam.

Flying Footnotes

The first person to actually fly solo around the world was the American aviator Wiley Hardeman Post, an experienced high altitude pilot. Flying a Lockheed Vega he completed the circumnavigation in 1933 taking seven days and nineteen hours to complete the journey.

The first woman to achieve the feat solo was Geraldine 'Gerry' Mock aboard a Cessna 180 aircraft called the Spirit of Columbus. She completed the circuit on April 18th, 1964. It took her almost twenty-nine and a half days.

Amelia Earhart

Map showing route followed by Amelia Earhart on her final flight finishing near Howland Island

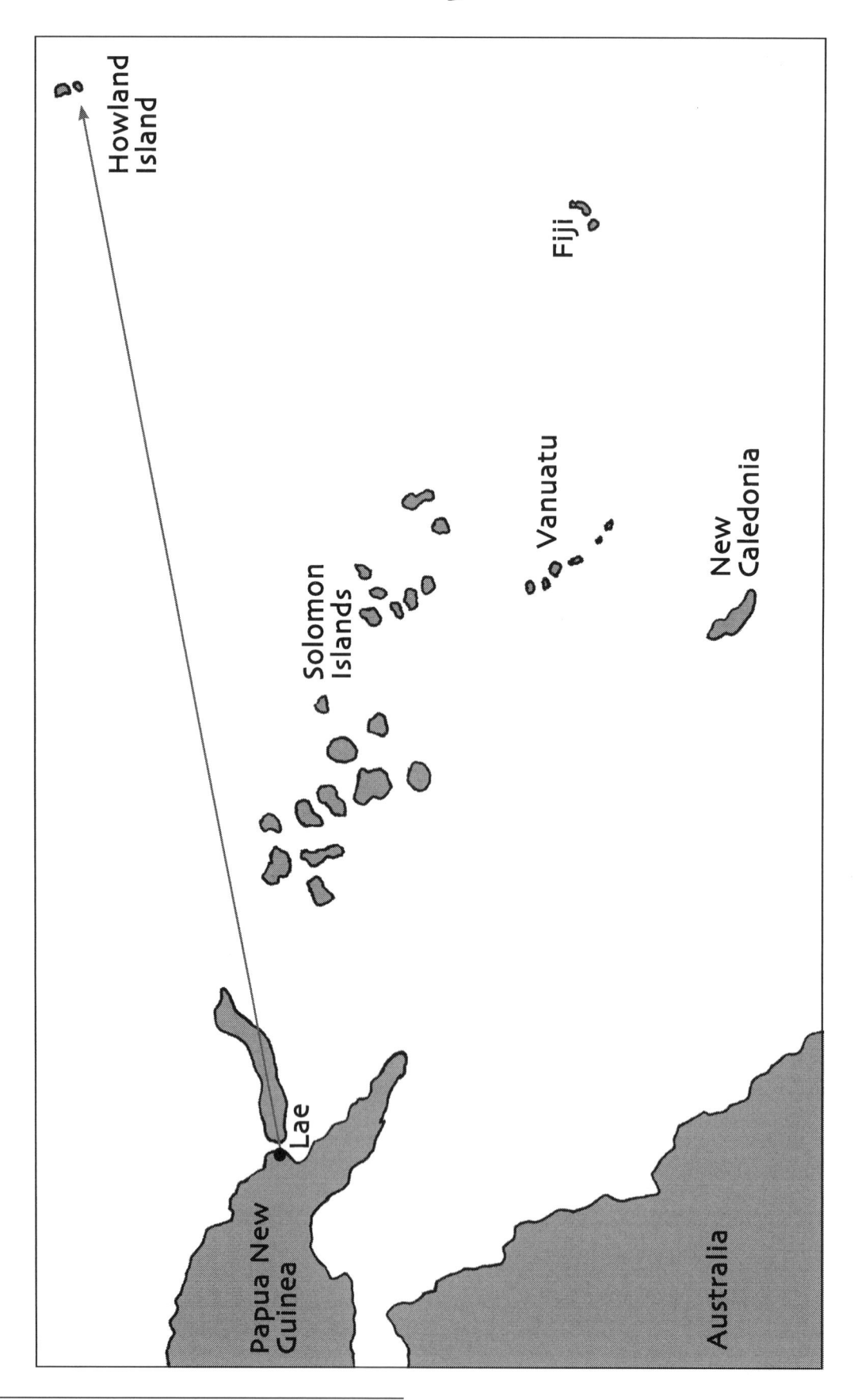

Then...

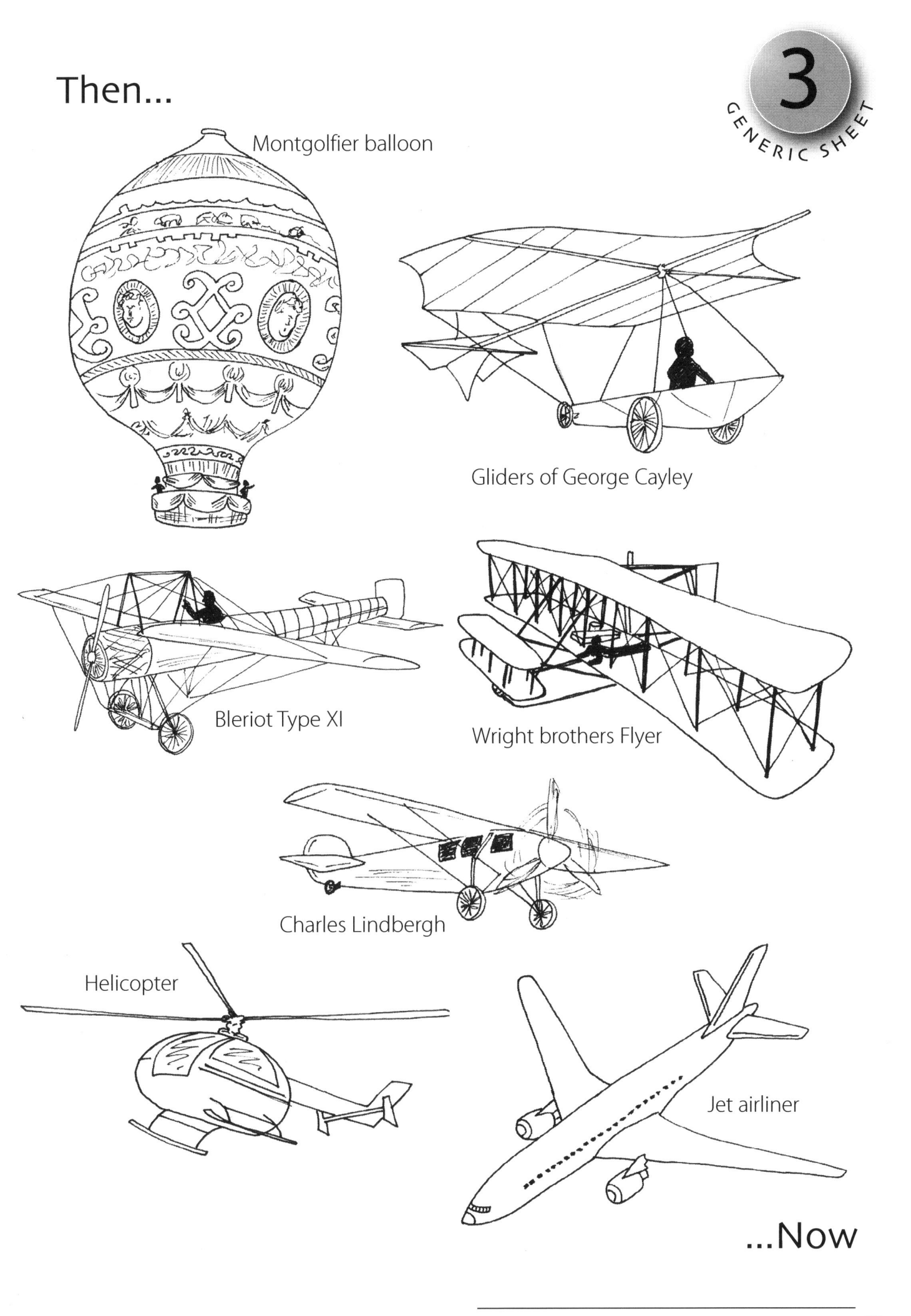

Montgolfier balloon

Gliders of George Cayley

Bleriot Type XI

Wright brothers Flyer

Charles Lindbergh

Helicopter

Jet airliner

...Now

GENERIC SHEET 3

CURRICULUM FOCUS • Famous journeys 13

Amelia Earhart quotes

Adventure is worthwhile in itself.

Women must try to do things men have tried. When they fail, their failure must be but a challenge to others.

Preparation, I have often said, is two-thirds of any venture.
Never do things others can do or will do, if there are things others cannot do and will not do.

Better to do a good deed near at home than go far away to burn incense.

Courage is the price that life exacts for granting peace.
The soul that knows it not, knows no release from little things.

Worry retards reaction and makes clear-cut decisions impossible.

In my life I had come to realise that when things were going very well indeed it was just the time to anticipate trouble. And conversely, I learned from pleasant experience that at the most desperate crisis, when all looked sour beyond words, some delightful break was apt to lurk around the corner.

The woman who can create her own job is a woman who will win fame and fortune.

No kind action ever stops itself. One kind action leads to another.
Good example is followed. A single act of kindness throws out roots in all directions and the roots spring up and makes new trees. The greatest work that kindness does to others is that it makes them kind themselves.

The most difficult thing is the decision to act; the rest is merely tenacity.
The fears are paper tigers. You can do anything you decide to do. You can act to change and control your life; and the procedure, the process, is its own reward.

Flying may not be all plain sailing but the fun of it is worth the price.

Anticipation, I suppose, sometimes exceeds realisation.

Amelia Earhart questions and answers

When was Amelia Earhart born?

Amelia was born on July 24th, 1897.

Where was she born?

She was born at the home of her grandfather, Alfred Otis, in the town of Atchison, Kansas.

What family did she have?

Her father, Edwin Earhart was a lawyer but he worked at a number of different jobs including as clerk of a railway company while Amelia was growing up. Her mother was called Amy and Amelia had a younger sister called Muriel. Both girls had nicknames. Amelia was known as Meeley or Millie while Muriel was usually called Pidge.

What hobbies did Amelia have when she was young?

Both Amelia and her sister liked outdoor activities like riding, skating and shooting. They caught creatures like moths, butterflies, toads and frogs and kept them as pets. With the help of an uncle and Muriel, Amelia built a curved wooden track from the roof of a shed to the ground. She made a small cart and would ride on this down the track.

Where and when did she see her first aircraft?

Amelia saw her first aeroplane at the Iowa State Fair at Des Moines in 1908 when she was eleven years old. She was not impressed and thought it was just a tangle of rusty wire and wood.

Why did Amelia go to Canada?

Amelia went to visit her sister Muriel who had moved to live in Toronto.

What did she do there?

She spent almost a year working in a military hospital as a nursing aide. The hospital was treating Canadian soldiers who had been injured fighting in the First World War. She scrubbed floors and handed out medicine and food. She had to work long hours and grew pale and thin. Her nursing job finished when the war ended in November 1918.

When and where did Amelia make her first flight?

It was late in 1920 that Amelia made her first flight while she was visiting an air show at Long Beach, California. Wearing a helmet and goggles that had been given to her she flew over Los Angeles. The flight lasted about ten minutes and cost her father $10.

Who trained her to become a pilot?

She took flying lessons with Anita 'Neta' Snook who owned a Canuck, an old Canadian training plane. Amelia had to save the money to pay for lessons. To look the part she bought a leather jacket and cut her hair short in the style of other female flyers. She picked up things quickly and hung around the airfield finding out how aeroplanes worked.

What was Amelia's first aircraft called?

After more saving, Amelia was able to buy her first aircraft. It was a bright yellow Kinner Airster bi-plane that she nicknamed 'The Canary'. There were a number of small crashes in this aircraft but by the end of 1921 Amelia was able to make her first solo flight.

What record did she set in October 1922?

Earhart flew the Airster to a height of 14000 feet (4300 metres), setting a world altitude record for female pilots.

What phone call changed her life in 1926?

While at work one afternoon Amelia got a telephone call from Captain Hilton Railey. He asked the question, 'How would you like to be the first woman to fly across the Atlantic Ocean?' He had been asked to find someone to carry out the journey by George Putnam.

Who was George Putnam?

George Putnam was a New York publisher who liked to specialise in real-life adventures. He was looking for a woman who knew about flying but also a person who would be confident enough to handle the publicity and fame that would follow. Once he interviewed Amelia he knew that she would be the one.

Who took Amelia across the Atlantic in 1928?

Two pilots, Wilmer Stultz and Louis Gordon flew the three-motor Fokker aircraft called Friendship across the Atlantic. Amelia was given the title of flight commander and it was her job to keep a record of the flight. They faced darkness, fog and snow during the flight that lasted for twenty hours, forty minutes.

Where did the aircraft land?

The Friendship, which was fitted with floats so that it could take off and land on water, took off from Newfoundland in Canada and came down just off the coast of South Wales near Burry Port. It had originally intended to land in Ireland.

What celebrations were held when the three fliers got back to America?

There was a ticker tape welcome in New York. They drove through the streets in an open car and ticker tape, small pieces of torn paper, flooded down on them from tall buildings rather like a snowstorm. This was followed by a reception at the White House in Washington with the President, Calvin Coolidge.

When did Amelia's solo flight over the Atlantic take place?

The first solo flight took place in May 1932. It was the fifth anniversary of the first solo Atlantic crossing by another American, Charles Lindbergh in his aircraft Spirit of St. Louis. Amelia again used Newfoundland as her starting point.

What aircraft did she use this time?

For this flight, Amelia was flying a Lockheed Vega. During the flight her altimeter stopped working so she could not tell how high she was. She flew through a storm, the wings iced up and flames came from a cracked exhaust pipe. Despite all these problems, she landed safely at Derry in Northern Ireland.

How long did the flight take?

The flight lasted for fourteen hours and fifty-six minutes. As a result of the flight Amelia was awarded several special gold medals and there was another hero's welcome when she went back to America.

How did the first flight around the world fail?

Now flying a Lockheed Electra 10E, Amelia was attempting to be the first woman to fly around the world and the first to travel by the longest distance possible. The aeroplane travelled successfully from America to Hawaii in the Pacific but it crashed when trying to take off from Luke Field, Pearl Harbour, Hawaii. It was badly damaged and was sent back to America for repairs.

Who was her navigator on the second attempt?

Her navigator on the second attempt would be Fred Noonan. He was a trusted navigator with particular experience flying over the Pacific Ocean.

Name some of the places they stopped on the world flight.

The aircraft travelled from east to west on this journey in 1937, roughly following the line of the equator. They landed first at Puerto Rico and then on to Africa and the Red Sea. Then there were stops at Karachi, Calcutta, Rangoon, Bangkok, Singapore, Bandung on the island of Java, Port Darwin, Australia and Lae, New Guinea.

How far had they flown when they reached Lae?

The aircraft was about three-quarters of its way through the journey, 3500km had already been covered and there was still 1100km to go.

Where did the aircraft disappear?

The aircraft left Lae on July 2nd. Watchers saw the Electra for the last time as it flew into the clouds. Its destination was the tiny Howland Island in the Pacific Ocean. The last messages were received in the early hours of July 3rd but then there was silence.

Who helped in the search for Amelia?

A huge search and rescue mission was launched to try to find the missing aircraft. Nine naval ships and over sixty aeroplanes were used. Ships searched for wreckage and planes flew over uninhabited islands looking for signs of life. Later George Putnam organised his own private search but still nothing was found.

When was Amelia officially declared dead?

In order that George Putnam could deal with her estate and settle bills, Amelia Earhart was officially declared dead in January 1939.

What reasons have been given to explain the disappearance of the aircraft?

The most fanciful theories say that Amelia could have been on a spying mission or that she was captured and executed by the Japanese on the island of Saipan. One idea, suggested later in a book, said she had gone back to America, changed her name and remarried.

What is the most likely explanation?

The most likely explanation for the disappearance is that the aircraft ran out of fuel trying to find the location of Howland Island and crashed into the sea.

Why did Amelia Earhart become such a well-known celebrity?

Flying was still very much in its infancy when Amelia became a pilot. It was also unusual in those times for women to fly aircraft and even more so to take them on high altitude and long distance flights. She became a hero to the people all over the world because she was prepared to try to break new records and push the limits.

What special qualities did she show during her flying?

She displayed characteristics like courage, coolness under pressure, perseverance and determination. She always wanted to achieve the things she set out to do even though there were often setbacks on the way. He views are shown in a letter she wrote to George Putnam during the last flight. 'Please know that I am quite aware of the hazards. I want to do it because I want to do it. Women must try to do things as men have tried. When they fail their failure must be but a challenge to others.'

LESSON PLAN 1

Famous flier

History objectives
- To find out who Amelia Earhart was and what she did.
- To find out why she became famous.

Resources

- A large picture of Amelia Earhart.
- A class timeline
- A large map of the United States of America.
- A large map of the world.
- Activity sheets 1-3
- Generic sheets 1, 4, 5-7.

Starting point: whole class

Talk about famous people who are currently in the news. They could be singers, dancers, sports personalities, television stars, politicians, fashion celebrities etc. Ask:

- Why are they famous?
- How did they become famous?
- How long have they been famous?
- Did they deserve to become famous?
- Will there be a time when they won't be famous any more? How might this happen?
- Have they done anything so important that it will become a key event in history?

Compare the cases of people who win televised talents competitions, for example, and become famous almost overnight. Ask:

- Is it right they should become famous so quickly?
- How did they earn their fame? Are they able to cope with the success or does it cause problems?

Talk with the children about how they would feel to become a famous person. Ask:

- What would they most like to succeed at?
- How would they spend their time?
- Would fame bring them lots of money?
- How would they spend it?
- Should people who are famous behave in a certain way?

Explain to children that eighty years ago in the 1930s there were no televisions and people's fame only spread through newspaper reports, radio and film. When these famous people lived in other countries, apart from Britain, it often took a long time for the news to travel about what they had done and achieved. There were no twenty-four hour news bulletins so it often took several days or even longer for details of important events to spread.

Then show them a picture or photograph of Amelia Earhart, preferably in her flying gear, see Generic sheet 1. Tell them she was a famous aviator who was born in 1897 and is thought to have died in 1937. Show them where 1900 and 1930 would be on the class timeline. Amelia would have become famous during the lifetime of the children's great-grandparents. Say she was one of the first women to fly and that she broke records for flying at altitude (height in the sky) and long distance. Encourage them to talk about Amelia's picture. Ask:

- What sort of hairstyle does she have?
- What sort of clothes is she wearing?
- How are they different from the clothes we wear today?
- Why does she need to wear special clothing?
- Does anyone know her name and why she became famous?

Tell children that Amelia Earhart became interested in flying when she was a teenager and took lessons so that she could qualify as a trained pilot. Display a large-scale map of North America pointing out some of the locations connected with her life. These might include Kansas where she was born, Iowa where she saw her first aircraft, Long Beach, California where she took her first flight, Newfoundland where she started her trans-Atlantic flights and New York where she enjoyed ticker tape welcomes.

Use the questions and answers on Generic sheet 5 to help build up some background information about the life of Amelia Earhart.

Tell children that Amelia was invited to make the first crossings of the Atlantic Ocean in an aeroplane by the New York publisher George Putnam who later became her husband. Display a large-scale map of the world showing the routes she followed in the two flights across the Atlantic i.e. from Newfoundland to South Wales (with others) and from Newfoundland to Northern Ireland (solo). Show the routes of some of her other early flights e.g. Hawaii to California and Los Angeles to Mexico City. Highlight the dangers of making any kind of long-distance flight at this time especially solo ones.

Use the questions and answers on Generic sheets 4, 5, 6 and 7 to add to the information about Amelia's early long-distance solo flights and some of the things she said about her exploits.

Group activities

Activity sheet 1
On this activity sheet, children who need support are given six main events to place in the correct sequence on the timeline. Focus more on getting the sequence of events correct rather than checking the arrows are placed in exactly the right position. Talk about the fact that Amelia was born in the nineteenth century (1800s) but that the rest of the key events occur in the twentieth century (1900s). Emphasise the use of important 'historical' vocabulary like 'before', 'after' and 'about the same time as.'

Activity sheet 2
These children have to put eight events into the right sequence on the timeline. Explain to children that timelines can run vertically or horizontally but that the version they are working with here is usually known as the 'winding road.' Although the timeline twists and turns, ensure all labelling is written horizontally in the usual way and that dates are clearly marked with an arrow. Discuss with children how the timeline is marked in decades (periods of ten years) and how it shows both the nineteenth (1800s) and the twentieth (1900s) centuries.

Activity sheet 3
More able children are provided with ten events in the life of Amelia Earhart in mixed order and have to devise, draw and label the timeline they intend to use. Discuss the three main possibilities, vertical, horizontal and winding road, although they may have alternative suggestions of their own. They may know of other events from the story of Amelia Earhart that they want to include. Make sure these children are familiar with words like 'decade', 'century' and 'millennium'.

Plenary session

Revise the content of the lesson with a role-play session in which you, a helper or another adult plays the part of Amelia Earhart. Respond to the children's questions by trying to provide some of the reasoning behind the things that Amelia did. Questions might include the following:

- When were you born?
- When did you first become interested in aircraft?
- When did you first fly? How did it feel?
- What was it like flying solo across the Atlantic?
- What dangers did you face?
- How did people celebrate when you broke a record?
- What was it like being called a hero?
- What were the main problems of being famous?
- Of the aircraft you flew, which was your favourite?
- Why did you want to fly around the world?

Ideas for support

Helping primary aged children to develop a greater awareness of time is one of the most difficult parts of teaching history. Focus in the time-lining activity on getting the sequence of events correct. Also help children calculate the periods of time that elapsed between each of the major events. Children working on Activity sheet 3 may need some help deciding what form of timeline to use and the best way of setting down a scale.

Ideas for extension

Find out more about the celebrations that were held when Amelia successfully achieved a record-breaking flight. By the age of 35 she was one of the best-known women in America. What are the origins of a ticker tape welcome through the streets of downtown New York? What special medals were awarded to Amelia Earhart? Which Presidents of the United States of America was she introduced to? Which President's wife did she become particularly good friends with?

Famous Flier

Name ....

Here are some of the main events in the life of Amelia Earhart.

Put them in the correct sequence on the timeline below. Use arrows to show their position and label each one carefully.

Events to be arranged

1928 Solo Atlantic flight

1908 Saw first aeroplane

1937 Round world flight attempt

1920 First aircraft flight

1931 Marries George Putnam

1897 Born in Atchison, Kansas

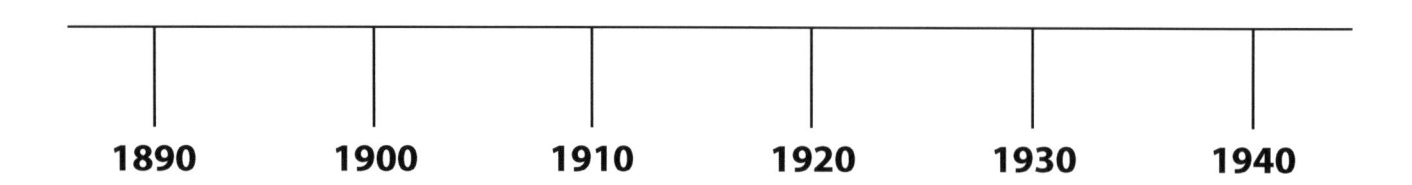

| 1890 | 1900 | 1910 | 1920 | 1930 | 1940 |

CURRICULUM FOCUS • Famous journeys

Famous Flier

Name ....

Put some of the main events in the life of Amelia Earhart in the right sequence on the 'winding road' timeline shown below.

Show each date clearly with an arrow and label each one carefully.

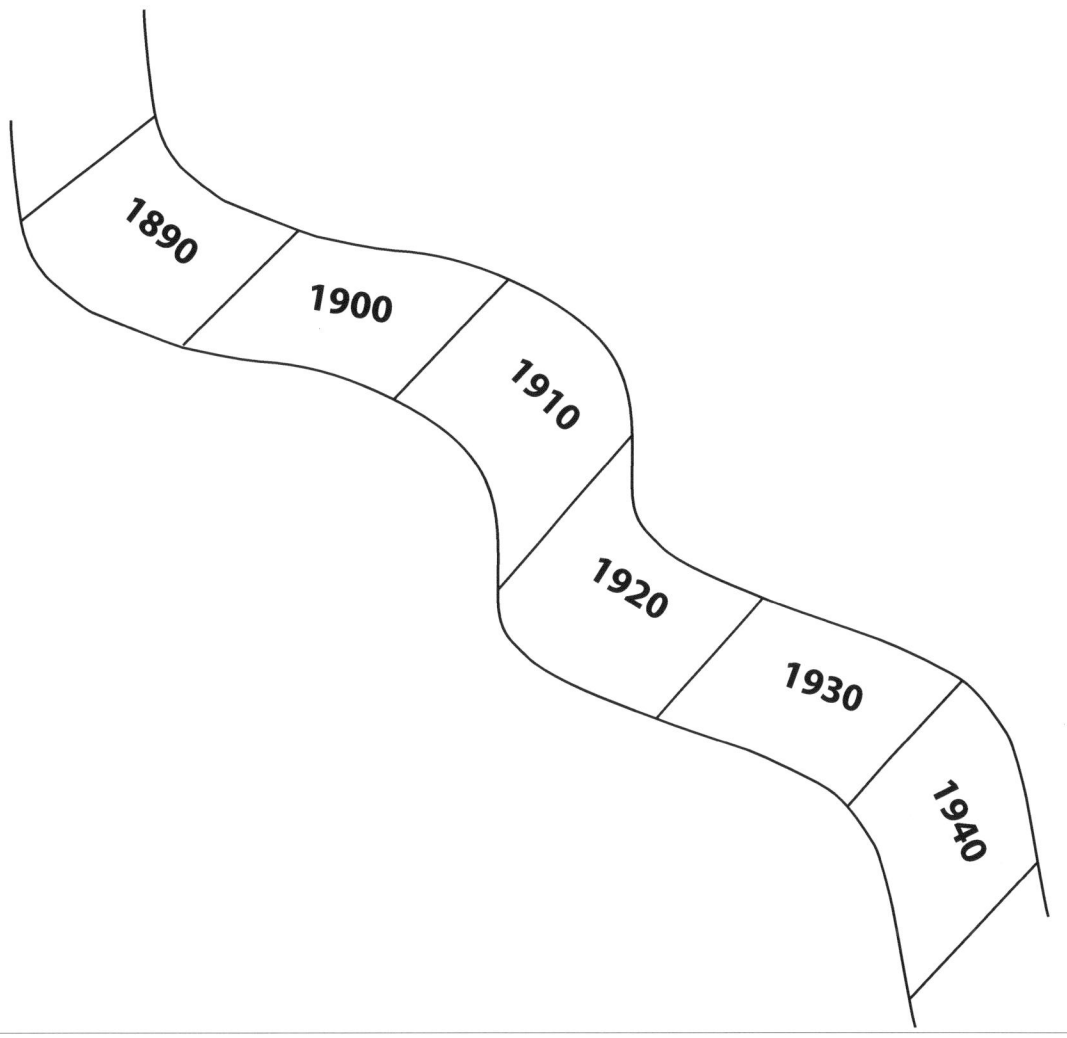

[Winding road timeline with decade markers: 1890, 1900, 1910, 1920, 1930, 1940]

1932	Solo Atlantic flight	1920	First aeroplane ride
1908	Saw first aeroplane	1897	Born in Atchison, Kansas
1928	First woman to fly the Atlantic	1931	Marries George Putnam
1937	Round world flight and disappearance	1922	First altitude record

CURRICULUM FOCUS • Famous journeys 21

Famous Flier

Name ....

Ten of the most important events in the life of Amelia Earhart are given below with the dates when they happened.

Draw a timeline to show these events using any style you think is suitable. Use an appropriate scale and position the events in the correct sequence.

1932 Solo Atlantic flight	1937 Disappears on world flight
1935 Hawaii to USA flight	1918 Nursing in Canada
1922 First altitude record	1928 First woman to fly Atlantic
1897 Born in Atchison, Kansas	1908 Saw first aeroplane
1931 Marries George Putnam	1920 First air trip

Last flight

2 LESSON PLAN

History objectives
- To follow the route flown by Amelia Earhart on her last flight.
- To investigate what might have happened to Amelia Earhart.

Resources

- Large pictures/photographs of Amelia Earhart
- World maps
- Detailed maps of the region around Australia
- Copies of daily newspapers
- Activity sheet 1-3
- Generic sheets 6-7

Starting points: whole class

Talk about the circumstances leading up to Amelia Earhart's last flight in 1937. Plans first started to be made two years before as such record-breaking attempts take a long time to organise. Discuss some of the preparations needed including choosing a new aircraft, planning the route, deciding on helpers, arranging stopover locations etc. Explain how they were forced to do all of this in secret so that other female pilots did not find out about it and make attempts themselves.

Talk about Amelia's motivation for making the flight. Consider the following possibilities. She was getting older and wanted a new challenge. She wanted to be the first and beat everyone else. She was no longer in the limelight and wanted to be very famous again. This was one of the few major flying records that had not yet been broken. Amelia was aware of the danger and knew that the flight might fail. She told a reporter, 'I won't feel completely cheated if I fail to come back.'

Tell children about the ill-fated first attempt to fly around the world that ended in a crash. Tell them about the flight, going west across the Pacific, from California to Hawaii. Joining Amelia were navigator Fred Noonan, Harry Manning and stunt pilot Paul Mantz, who was acting as technical advisor. The flight to Hawaii took almost sixteen hours and they landed safely. However, when they attempted to take off again, the Lockheed Electra crashed badly damaging a wing and a wheel. The aircraft had to be taken back to America by sea so that repairs could be carried out.

Explain how the failed attempt only made Amelia more determined to fly around the world. The aircraft had to be repaired and more money had to be raised. Three months later, on June 1st, the team were ready to try again. This time Fred Noonan was to be Amelia's only companion and the flight would go in the opposite direction, leaving the long Pacific crossing until last.

On the world map, plot the route followed by Amelia on the second attempt. The aircraft flew across America from Oakland, California via Miami to Puerto Rico. From there to the north east coast of South America with stops at Caripito (Venezuela), Paramaribo (Surinam) and Natal (Brazil). After crossing the Atlantic Ocean to Africa calls were made to Dakar (Senegal), N'Djamena (Chad) and Khartoum (Sudan). Once over the Red Sea and across Saudi Arabia, calling points then included Karachi (Pakistan), Calcutta (India), Yangdon (Myanmar), Singapore, Java, Darwin (Australia) and Lae (Papua, New Guinea). Tell children that at this stage the flight had taken a month. A total of 3500km had been flown but there was still 1100km to go.

Use the questions and answers on Generic sheets 6 and 7 to find out what happened next once the Lockheed Electra left Lae and headed for the next stop at Howland Island.

Again, using the Generic sheets, discuss some of the explanations given for Amelia Earhart's disappearance once the aircraft left Lae including landing on an uninhabited island or being captured while spying. Which do children think is the most likely explanation? Do they think there could have been another cause of the disappearance? Ask them to give reasons for their choice.

Group activities

Activity sheet 1
Provide children working on this activity sheet with as much information about the disappearance of Amelia Earhart as possible. Discuss the final stages of the round the world flight with them so they are able to answer the questions fully. Help and support them with the final question where they have to give their own account of what they think might have happened. Explain that the next step would have been a flight to Hawaii. Encourage children to draw up their own lists of words for inclusion in the second task.

Activity sheet 2
Suitable maps and atlases will be needed for children who are working on this activity sheet. Ensure children put place names in the correct positions. Use a bright coloured pencil to mark in the route followed from Darwin to Lae and then from Lae towards Howland Island. Explain that the next step would have been a flight to Hawaii. Encourage children

CURRICULUM FOCUS • Famous journeys 23

to draw up their own lists of words for inclusion in the second task.

Activity sheet 3
More able children should study reports of Amelia Earhart's disappearance in some detail. The Internet may be a useful source of extra information. Display a selection of front pages of several daily and weekly newspapers in the classroom so children have some idea of the importance of layout and page design. Stress the need to get a good balance on the front page of illustrations and written text.

Plenary session

Choose suitable children to argue the case for each of the main reasons given for the disappearance of Amelia Earhart, Fred Noonan and the aircraft. Then discuss each one with the class and encourage children to cross-examine the 'witness' in courtroom style. Put it to the vote and see which of the various theories has the greatest support. Review in more general terms whether it was too dangerous to try a round the world flight at this time when aircraft and their engines could still be unreliable.

Ideas for support

Give plenty of help when children are plotting the route Amelia Earhart followed on her round the world flight. Emphasise how she was attempting to make the longest flight by sticking as close to the equator as possible. Explain terms like equator, continents, time zones, oceans etc. Assist with the construction of the pieces of writing required. Talk about the use of sentences combining several clauses and stress the use of good verbs and adjectives.

Ideas for extension

Talk about how the sun rises in the east and sets in the west. Navigators like Fred Noonan used the sun to work out directions during the day. At night they used the stars. Discuss the early use of radio for communication in aircraft like the Lockheed Electra. Morse code uses dots and dashes that can be tapped out to send messages. Different combinations stand for different numbers and letters. Find out about the disappearance of another famous woman pilot, Britain's Amy Johnson, while flying an aircraft solo over the River Thames in 1941. Investigate other strange disappearances at sea especially in the region known as The Bermuda Triangle.

Last flight

Name ....

Find out about the mystery surrounding the disappearance of Amelia Earhart's aircraft and then answer the following questions.

1. What type of aircraft was Amelia flying?

   _____
   _____

2. Who was the navigator on the flight?

   _____
   _____

3. From where did the aircraft leave on its last flight?

   _____
   _____

4. Where was Amelia trying to reach?

   _____
   _____

5. How did the fliers keep in touch with the ground?

   _____
   _____

6. What do you think happened to the Lockheed Electra?

   _____
   _____

Word bank
air sea island rescue search ships aircraft vessels radio navy warships fuel

Last flight

Name ....

This map shows the last journey made by Amelia Earhart on her round the world flight in 1937.

Label the following place names: Australia, Darwin, Pacific Ocean, Papua New Guinea, Lae, Howland Island, Hawaii.

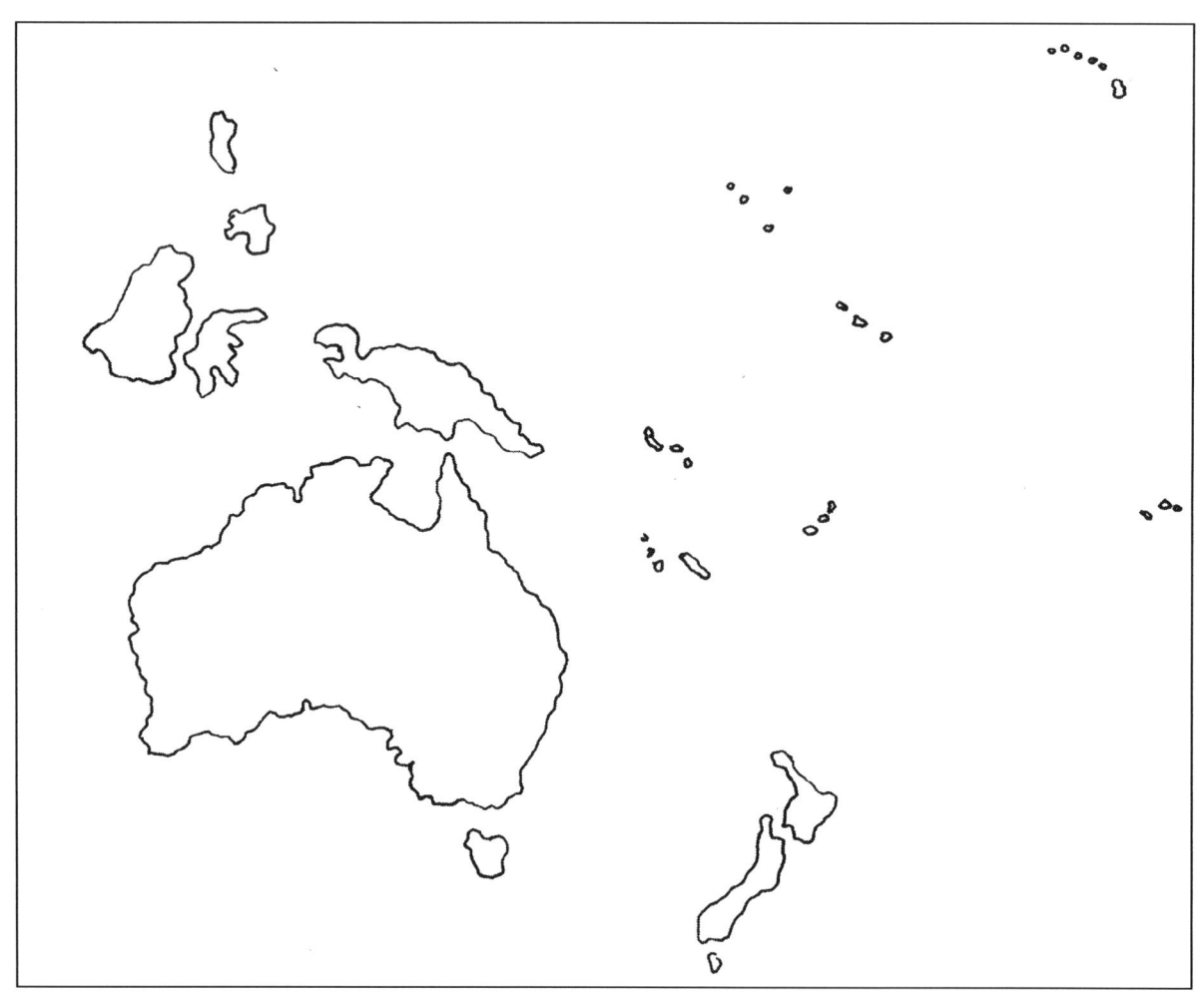

Explain in your own words what you think happened to Amelia Earhart, Fred Noonan and the Lockheed Electra.

_____

_____

_____

_____

26   CURRICULUM FOCUS • Famous journeys

Last flight

ACTIVITY SHEET 3

Name ....

Find out as much as you can about the last journey made by Amelia Earhart during the round the world flight in 1937.

Then write up the story in your own words, with illustrations, for the local newspaper in the town where Amelia was born, Atchison, Kansas.

Explain in the article what you think might have happened.

Kansas Chronicle

September 12th 1937

CURRICULUM FOCUS • Famous journeys 27

LESSON 3

Air travel

History objectives
- To investigate the early development of flight.
- To consider how powered flight has evolved during the last one hundred years.

Resources

- Generic sheet 3
- Pictures and photographs of early flight pioneers
- Pictures and photographs of modern jet aircraft
- Activity sheets 1-3
- Cardboard and paper of different thickness
- Tissue paper
- Scissors and glue
- Paper clips, string, straws
- Hair drier

Before the history lesson

Undertake some design and technology lessons that will help children appreciate the basic principles behind the reasons why aircraft are able to fly. Also the problems early pioneers had to overcome when building and piloting primitive aircraft. They should design, construct and test their own simple models.

Hot air balloons

Try this method of making a hot air balloon. Lay six large sheets of tissue paper on top of each other and on the top sheet draw the outline of a balloon panel. Cut these out and fold each of the panels separately. Glue the panels together carefully making sure the glue does not spread further than the seam. Newspaper will help here. Link the two ends together and leave plenty of time for drying. To help the shape of the balloon, make and add a thin collar at the base and a large disc at the top to give added strength. Thin card is better for these items. See Figure 1. A hair dryer will provide a good supply of warm air but allow the balloon time to fill up before testing inside or outdoors on a calm day.

- How long does it take the balloon to rise?
- How far does it travel?
- Does it rise or fall quickly or slowly?
- Experiment with balloons of different sizes. Do large balloons stay in the air longer?

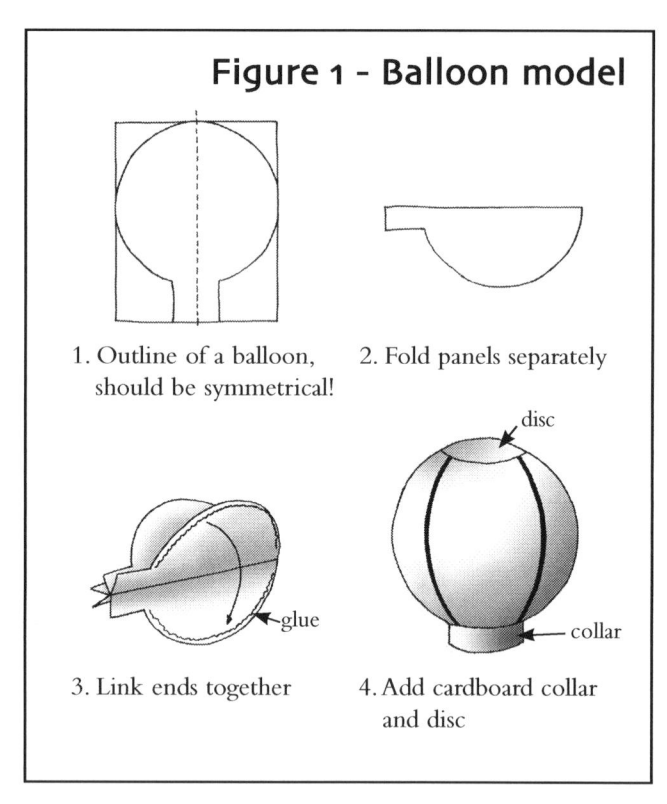

Figure 1 - Balloon model

1. Outline of a balloon, should be symmetrical!
2. Fold panels separately
3. Link ends together
4. Add cardboard collar and disc

Uplifting wings

Investigate the importance of wings in providing flying devices with sufficient lift to help get them off the ground. Using paper or thin cardboard make different shaped wings to see which will produce the most effective lift. Suspend the wing using thin string and a straw. Ask someone to blow

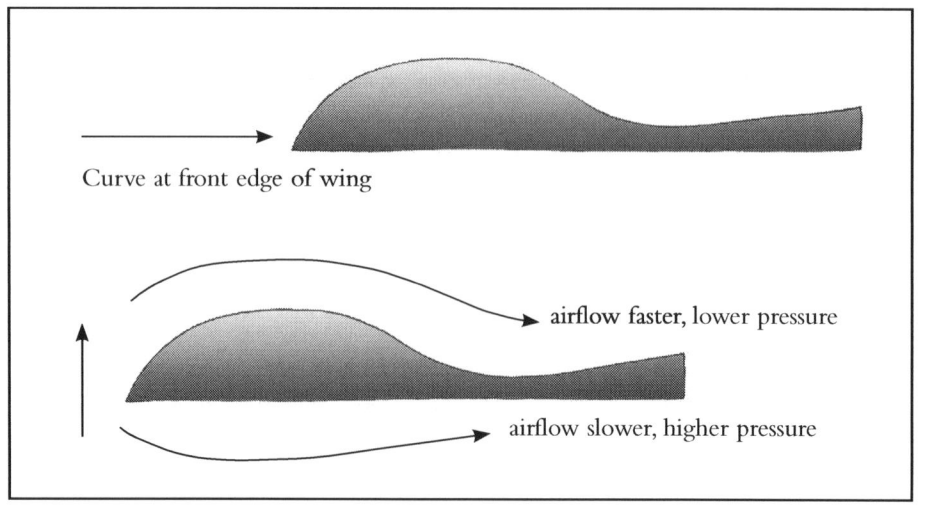

Curve at front edge of wing

airflow faster, lower pressure

airflow slower, higher pressure

across the top of the wing. Try to make a curve in the front edge of the wing. See Figure 2.

- What happens now?
- Is the curve better at the back?

Now make the wing three-dimensional and test again in various positions. It should become clear that the airflow is faster over the top of the curved wing than it is on the flatter lower part. Because the slower moving air at the bottom has a higher pressure, the wing is pushed up when the aircraft flies.

Paper darts

Move on to examine basic dart shapes folded from A4 sheets of paper or thin card. Encourage children to make the shape as streamlined as possible. Experiment with the design. Use paper clips to improve balance. Introduce tail flaps of some kind. See Figure 3.

- Does this help the paper dart fly longer and straighter?
- Does it fly better with the flaps up or down?
- What effect do side stabilisers have?

Time flights to establish which models are record breakers. Place the tail flaps in different positions.

- What effect does this have?

Now change the shape of the dart so that it becomes more Concorde style with swept back delta wings.

- Does this improve performance?

Point out to children that variables, like the speed of launching and the angle at which the dart is launched, will effect how it performs.

Important forces

While conducting these activities, look in more depth at the four important forces acting on an aircraft. They are drag, thrust, lift and gravity. The engine provides thrust while drag is the resistance of the air in flight. It acts in the opposite direction to the way in which the aircraft is moving. As mentioned before, the wings of the aircraft provide lift to counteract the force of gravity that attempts to pull it down.

Starting points: whole class

After the children have completed various models in the design and technology lessons, talk about how manned flight developed.

Leonardo da Vinci was making sketches of flying machines as early as 1485. Show pictures of the flight of the Montgolfier brothers, Jacques and Joseph, in a hot air balloon over Paris in 1783. See Generic sheet 3.

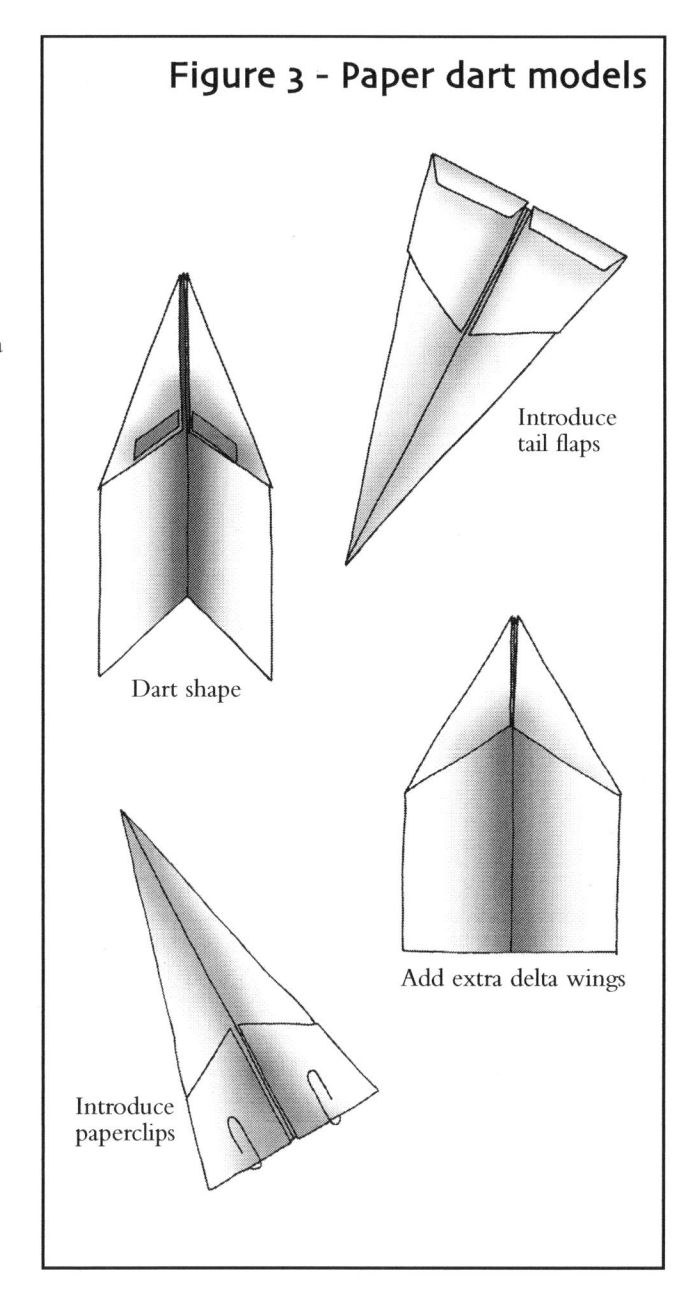

Figure 3 – Paper dart models

Dart shape

Introduce tail flaps

Add extra delta wings

Introduce paperclips

- What was the balloon filled with to make it rise?
- How far did it rise in the air?
- Who were the passengers carried in the balloon?

Investigate the work of the Englishman, George Cayley (1773-1857) who is often called the 'Father of Aviation'. He first developed piloted gliders and wrote about them in his famous book On Aerial Navigation. He invented the use of cambered wings on aircraft and was the first to recognise the importance of forces like gravity, drag, thrust and lift. See Generic sheet 3.

Move on to look at the beginnings of powered flight and the pioneering work done by Orville and Wilbur, the Wright brothers. They built and fitted a four-cylinder engine to their biplane glider. The engine powered two propellers and was flown by a pilot who lay across the lower wing and controlled the aircraft with a series of wires and levers. Called Flyer 1, the machine first flew in December 1903 at Kitty Hawk. It was in the air for twelve seconds, reached a height of three metres and flew a distance of thirty-six metres along the beach. See also Generic sheet 3. By 1905, this ever-improving flying machine was staying up for as long as forty minutes.

Group activities

Activity sheet 1
On this activity sheet children are provided with pictures of six different aircraft. These six pictures have to be sorted into 'then' and 'now' groups to illustrate the changes that have taken place in air travel. Scissors, glue and spare paper will be needed for cutting out the pictures, sorting them and sticking them ready for display.

Activity sheet 2
The same six pictures also have to be sorted into 'then' and 'now' on this activity sheet. In addition children have to write short sentences about each of the aircraft shown. A word bank is provided to help them formulate their ideas.

Activity sheet 3
On this activity sheet for more able children, only empty pictures boxes are provided. This time, using the details given in the captions and their own research, children have to draw their own pictures. Space is also provided at the bottom of the sheet for children to describe, in sentence form, the main changes that have taken place in aircraft design and propulsion over the last one hundred years.

Plenary session

Review the practical work carried out by the children making balloons, wings and paper darts. Find out what they know about why heavy aircraft are able to fly long distances through the air. Focus particularly on changes and amendments they made to the design of their models which helped to improve performance.

Assess the work children have carried out on the activity sheets highlighting the main ways in which air travel has developed over time. Compare and contrast changes to wing and fuselage shape, method of propulsion, pilot position and accommodation facilities for carrying passengers etc.

Ideas for support

Use as many good quality pictures and photographs as possible so that children are able to pick out detail on aircraft from both the present and the past. Encourage plenty of discussion initially so children begin to appreciate the main differences between 'then' and 'now'. It may also help to do some time-lining activities with aircraft pictures so children can see how one stage of change has developed into another. Some help with cutting, sticking and accurate labelling may be necessary for children working on Activity sheet 1 and Activity sheet 2.

Ideas for extension

Through research, look in more detail at the exploits of other pioneering fliers who attempted and established long-distance records. Focus especially on individuals like Louis Bleriot, the first person to fly across the English Channel (1909), John Alcock and Arthur Whitten Brown and Charles Lindbergh, first flights across the Atlantic (1919 and 1927) and Amy Johnson, Britain to Australia flight (1930).

- What sort of aircraft did these people use?
- Who provided financial backing or sponsorship to help them?
- How long did the flights last?
- Did they fly alone or were they helped?
- What particular dangers did they face?

Extend the practical activities to look at other aspects of flight including the principles used by helicopters (paper spinners) and jet aircraft (shooting a balloon along a stretch of nylon fishing line).

Air travel

Name ....

These are pictures of different types of aircraft. Which ones were flying in the past and which ones would you see flying today?

Cut out the pictures and sort them into two groups one showing 'Then' and the other 'Now'. Then stick them onto a fresh piece of paper.

Louis Bleriot aircraft

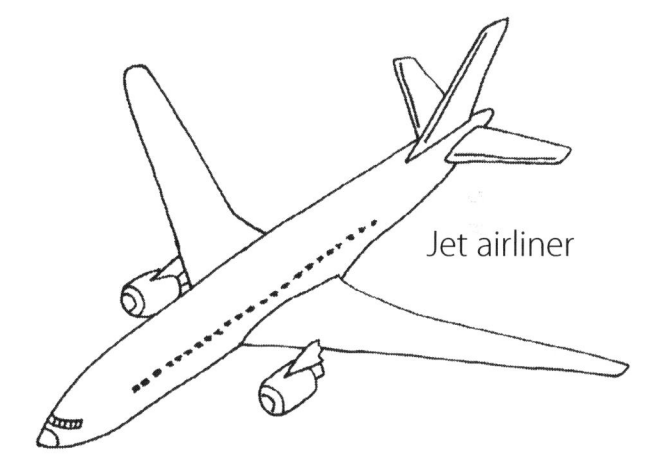

Jet airliner

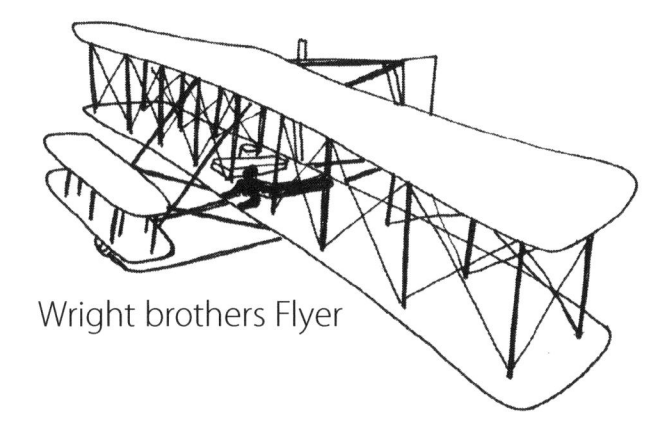

Wright brothers Flyer

Helicopter

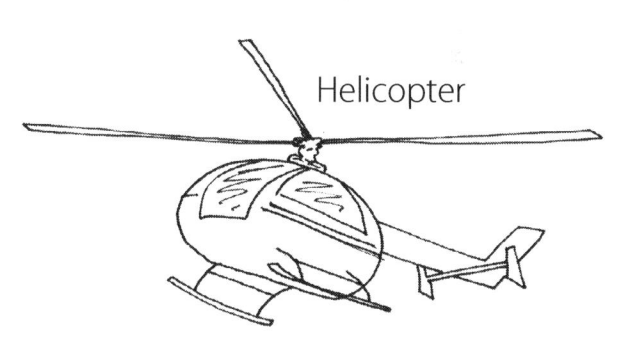

Hercules transport plane

Amelia Earhart aircraft

CURRICULUM FOCUS • Famous journeys 31

Air travel

Name ....

These are pictures of different aircraft. Which were flying in the past and which ones would you see today?

Cut out the pictures and sort them into two groups, one showing 'Then' and the other 'Now'.

Stick them on another piece of paper and write some short sentences about each one. There is a word bank to help you.

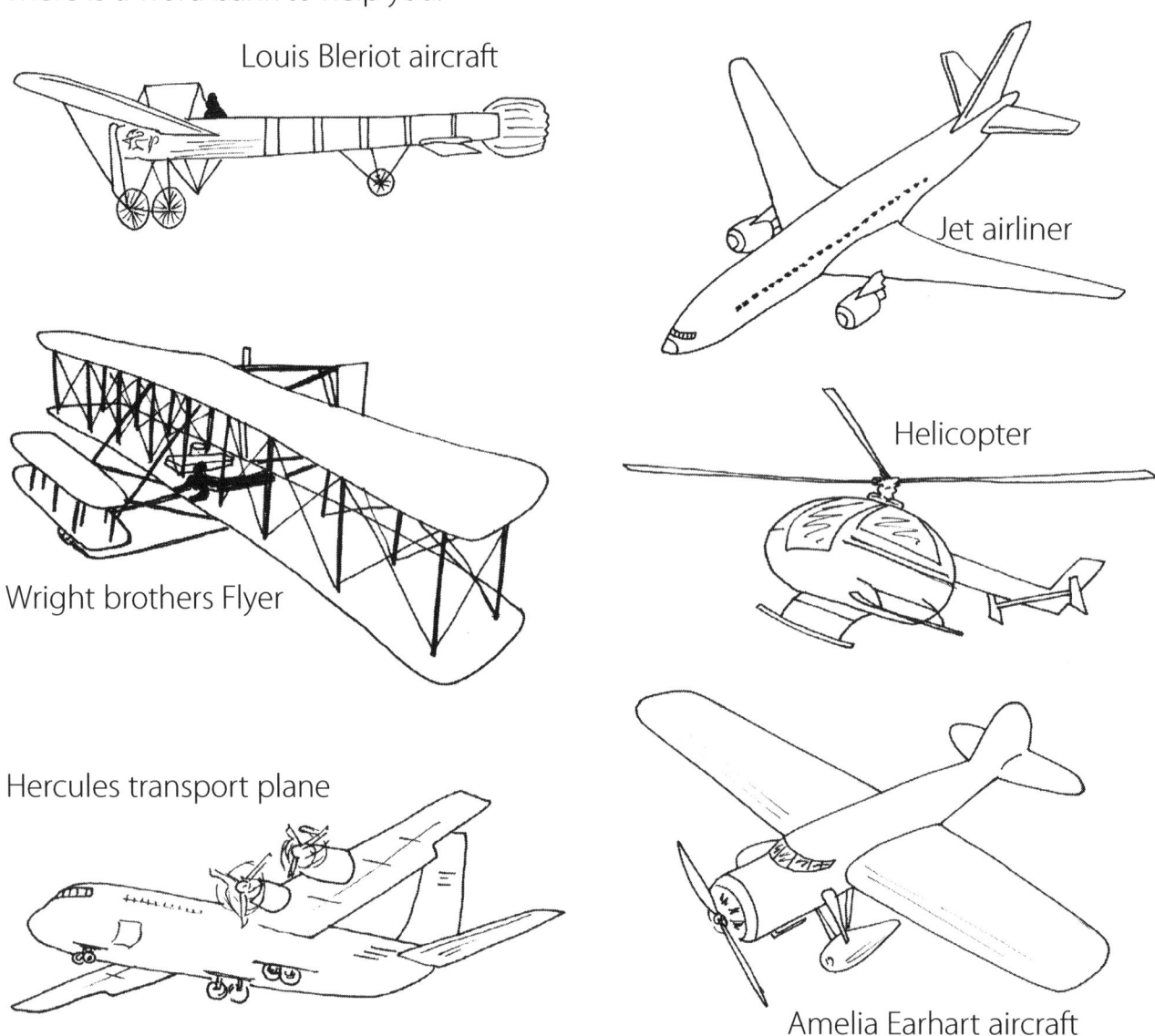

Louis Bleriot aircraft

Jet airliner

Wright brothers Flyer

Helicopter

Hercules transport plane

Amelia Earhart aircraft

Word bank
wings   fuselage   jet engine   petrol engine   propeller   pilot   passengers   controls
cockpit   fuel   streamlined

32   CURRICULUM FOCUS • Famous journeys

Air travel

Name ....

Draw pictures in the empty boxes to show the difference in aircraft between 'Then' and 'Now. The headings tell you what you should draw. Under each picture write some sentences to say what you have shown.

THEN: Wright brothers Flyer, Louis Bleriot aircraft and Amelia Earhart aircraft

NOW: Helicopter, Jet airliner and Hercules transport plane

Roald Amundsen

TEACHERS' NOTES

Off to sea

Roald Amundsen was born into a family of shipowners and sailors at Borge in Norway. His father and several uncles ran the company that specialised in exporting coal to China and timber to Britain and central Europe. Amundsen's father died when he was fourteen and his mother was anxious to keep him away from a life at sea. She pressurised him into becoming a doctor but he only kept the promise until his mother died. At that time, Amundsen, then aged twenty-one, quit university to spend his life travelling and exploring. He immediately joined the Norwegian navy and spent the following nine years with them studying science. Amundsen took his inspiration from fellow Norwegian explorer Fridtjof Nansen and the British sailor Sir John Franklin who had searched unsuccessfully for the North West Passage.

Amundsen's first major excursion came between 1897 and 1899 when he was made first mate on a ship called Belgica under the command of Adrien de Gerlache. It became the first expedition to spend a winter in the Antarctic. The ship was locked in sea ice off the coast of the frozen continent for a long period. It was a difficult time and the crew only survived because the expedition's doctor, Frederick Cook, prevented the men from catching scurvy by hunting animals like seal and penguin and feeding them fresh meat, an important lesson that Amundsen put to good use in his future expeditions.

North West Passage

By 1903 Amundsen had gained enough experience to be leading his own expeditions. In was in that year that he was in charge of a group of explorers that successfully crossed the Arctic's North West Passage linking the Atlantic and Pacific Oceans. It was a journey that sailors had been trying to complete since the fifteenth century. Amundsen and six others travelled in a steel protected seal-hunting vessel called Gjoa that had been fitted with a gasoline engine. The route they followed took them through Baffin Bay, Lancaster and Peel Sounds and the James Ross, Simpson and Rae Straits. Two winters were spent near King William Island where Amundsen learned about Arctic survival skills from the local people including the use of dog teams for pulling sledges and the benefit of wearing animal skins to keep warm. Following a third winter trapped in the ice, Amundsen and his team navigated into the Beaufort Sea and from there into the Bering Strait and the Pacific Ocean. At times during the voyage the depth of water was only one metre and a ship larger than the Gjoa would not have been successful.

Change of plans

Amundsen was keen to carry on exploring in the same region and began to formulate plans for an attempt to reach the North Pole. Trying to raise the necessary funds, however, took longer than expected. Then, after hearing that others, most notably the American explorer Robert Peary might have reached the North Pole, Amundsen decided to abandon his mission and turn south instead. He kept his plans as secret as he could not only from his own countrymen but also from the British explorer Robert Falcon Scott who was hoping to be the first person to reach the South Pole. Amundsen sailed south in the ship Fram (Forward) that had previously been used by one of his heroes, Nansen. They left Oslo, Norway's capital city, on June 3rd, 1910 and stopped at the island of Madeira in the Atlantic Ocean to take on fresh water and supplies. It was only when the Fram left Madeira that Amundsen was prepared to share the location of his eventual destination with the majority of his men. The Fram arrived at the edge of the Ross Ice Shelf in Antarctica on January 14th, 1911. Here Amundsen located his base camp and set about preparing for the trek to the Pole.

Reaching the South Pole

Amundsen had chosen to land in a region known as the Bay of Whales for a number of reasons. It was rich in animal life, especially seals and penguins, and this would give the men good supplies of fresh meat. It would also put the party some ninety kilometres closer to the South Pole. Unloading started straight away and base camp, a large prefabricated hut, was assembled. Food depots were established on the route to the Pole and on April 21st, when the sun finally went down, the party settled in for the long winter night.

By August 24th, the sun had reappeared but for two frustrating months the group was held up by bad weather. Tension built up as each day passed. Amundsen would have the men and dog sledges all prepared only to cancel the start at the last minute as the weather closed in. Finally on September 8th the weather relented and eight men with sledges pulled by over eighty dogs set off. By September 11th though, temperatures had plummeted to − 50 degrees Celsius. Compasses had frozen and Amundsen decided it was too dangerous to continue. They turned back to base and although the men got separated into pairs on the return journey they all made it safely.

On October 19th, a second attempt was made to reach the South Pole. This time the party consisted of Amundsen, Olav Bjaaland, Helmer Hanssen, Sverre Hassel and Oscar Wisting. They took four sledges to carry equipment and a total of fifty-two dogs. The men, using skis whenever possible, made good progress, averaging about thirty kilometres each day. They stopped at the depots that had been established previously where there were good supplies of food. On November 11th, the party spotted a range of mountains in the distance that Amundsen named Queen Maud's Range in honour of the Queen of Norway. They camped at the foot of the mountains to make final plans. There was a distance of some five hundred kilometres still to go before the pole was reached.

They climbed the Axel Heiberg Glacier before losing several days because of bad weather. They struggled on against driving snow in strong winds and thick fog. There was still a major obstacle to cross, a glacier with a thin crust of snow covering a number of dangerous and deep crevasses. By December 8th they had passed the furthest point south that the explorer Ernest Shackleton had reached and were within 140 kilometres of their goal. In mid-afternoon on Friday December 14th they called a halt as their sledge meter registered their arrival at the South Pole (90°00'S). That evening there were brief festivities in the tent while the five men shared a little seal meat. Several days were then spent double-checking their location using the position of the sun and readings were taken from numerous points around the pole. They also erected a tent proudly flying the Norwegian flag from its pole. Inside the tent they left a message for Scott and his party, who they suspected would not be far behind them, in addition to a letter to Norway's King Haakon. It took thirty-nine days for the party of men and the eleven remaining dogs to make the return journey. Then followed a frustrating month long voyage to the island of Tasmania where finally, on March 7th, the historic news was announced. Scott's group would arrive at the South Pole thirty-five days after Amundsen and would tragically lose their lives on the return journey to base camp. There were a number of important reasons why Amundsen's trek to the South Pole had proved successful. The expedition had been well planned and had used good equipment including the appropriate clothing. Amundsen and his team had a good understanding of dogs and how to handle them and they were expert skiers. In one of his books Amundsen wrote,' I may say this is the greatest factor-the way in which the expedition is equipped-the way in which every difficulty is foreseen and precautions taken for meeting or avoiding it. Victory awaits him who has everything in order-luck people call it. Defeat is certain for him who has neglected to take the necessary precautions in time; this is called bad luck.'

Back to the north

In 1918 Amundsen began an expedition in the new ship that had been built for him called Maud. He tried to sail through the North West Passage from west to east. Amundsen attempted to freeze the Maud into the polar ice cap so that it would drift towards the North Pole. He was not successful in doing this but the scientific evidence collected during the expedition proved to be invaluable.

By the beginning of the 1920s Amundsen was becoming frustrated by the fact that exploration in the Arctic region was forever hampered by frozen ice-bound seas. At the same time he began to take an interest in the rapid development of manned flight. It was not long then before the intrepid Norwegian started to investigate the possibility of overcoming his biggest problem by literally taking to the air. Flying not only meant that long distances could be covered more quickly but also provided an ideal way to accurately map the polar regions.

Up in the air

During 1923, Amundsen and Oskar Omdal of the Royal Norwegian Navy attempted to fly across the North Pole from Wainwright in Alaska to the island of Spitsbergen near Norway. The aircraft they were using became damaged in the flight and they were forced to abandon the journey.

Two years later Amundsen had another scheme to try. Accompanied by the American millionaire engineer Lincoln Ellsworth, a pilot and three other crew members, Amundsen took two Dornier flying boats to 87°44'N, the furthest north an aircraft had reached up until that time. The planes landed a few miles apart but despite the fact they were not in radio contact the crews managed to find each other. One of the aircraft was damaged but Amundsen and the others worked for over three weeks to clear an airstrip so they could take off from the ice. Finally the six people packed into the one good aircraft and with great skill the pilot flew it over the cracking ice to safety.

A new project was planned for 1926. Amundsen and a group of others including Lincoln Ellsworth, Oscar Wisting, one of the team that had reached the South Pole, and the Italian aeronautical engineer Umberto Nobile made the first crossing of the Arctic in an airship. The craft, called Norge and designed by Nobile, left Spitsbergen on May 11th, 1926 and landed in Alaska three days later. It had covered a distance of almost 5,500 kilometres and Norwegian, Italian and American flags were dropped as the airship flew over the North Pole. Despite the success, Amundsen and Nobile were to remain in dispute over who should really claim the credit for this achievement and who had actually been in charge of the expedition. One thing is certain however. If Peary was not successful in reaching the North Pole in 1909, then Amundsen and Wisting could claim to be the first persons to attain each geographical pole, by land or air.

The last flight

Amundsen set out on what was to be his last flight on June 11th, 1928 aboard a French built Latham 47 sea plane. With five others he went on a search and rescue mission to try to find the missing members of Nobile's crew. Nobile's new airship called the Italia had reportedly crashed while returning from a flight to the North Pole. Later a wing float and a fuel tank from Amundsen's Latham 47 were found but nothing of the six men. It is believed the aircraft crashed into the Barents Sea in fog somewhere between Bear Island and Tromso on the Norwegian mainland. Despite lengthy searches that lasted right into September, the bodies were never found. December 14th, 1928 was a national day of mourning for Amundsen in Norway-the anniversary of the day on which he had reached the South Pole. Ironically, Nobile was rescued from the pack ice on which he had been drifting and taken to safety while some of the other members of his crew were later picked up by a rescue ship. Six others remained missing, presumed dead. Nobile, who became a national hero in Italy for his exploits, went on to make other flights and eventually died in 1978 at the age of 93.

Both in 2004 and 2009 further searches were made by the Royal Norwegian Navy to try to locate the wreckage of Amundsen's Latham aircraft. The best and most up to date sonar systems were used including an unmanned submarine called Hugin 1000. The search focused on a large area of the sea floor where the sea plane is thought to have crashed. There were several interesting leads but no tangible results. It may be that the wrong location was searched. Scouring of the seabed by large fishing vessels may have removed wreckage from the site or the remains of the aircraft may have been completely destroyed by the massive amount of industrial fishing that has taken place in the area.

The legacy

Roald Amundsen is widely regarded as one of the greatest polar explorers. He excelled during the first twenty years of the twentieth century, a period of history often referred to as The Heroic Age of Polar Exploration. Amundsen travelled widely at both of the Earth's extremities covering huge distances at sea, on the land and in the air. Amundsen's account of his polar adventures can be read in his own words in several books including The South Pole: An account of the Norwegian Antarctic Expedition in the Fram, 1910-1912. The final stages of Amundsen's life and his relationship with Nobile is featured in the film The Red Tent which was released in 1969 starring Sean Connery and Peter Finch.

As a mark of his importance a number of places in both polar regions have been named after him. The Amundsen Sea, the Amundsen Glacier, Amundsen Bay and Mount Amundsen are all to be found in Antarctica. Amundsen Gulf is found in the Arctic Ocean and even a large crater covering the South Pole of the Moon is named after Amundsen.

Roald Amundsen

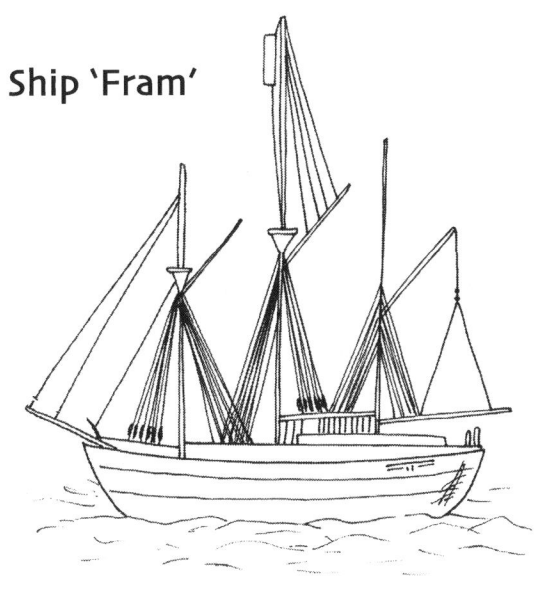

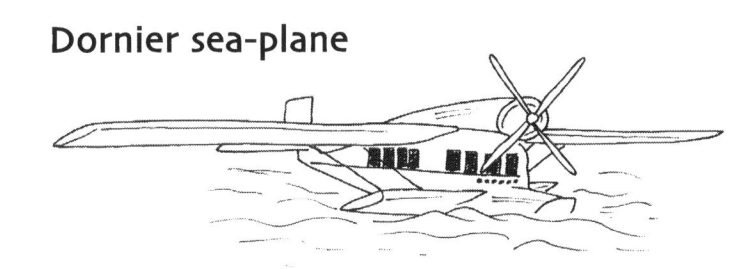

1 GENERIC SHEET

Ship 'Fram'

Dornier sea-plane

Airship 'Norge'

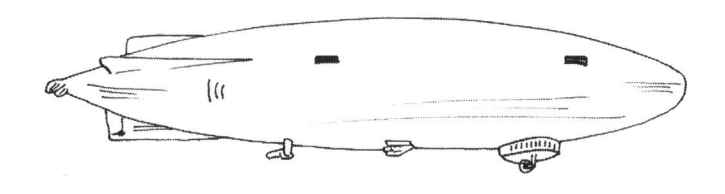

GENERIC SHEET 2

North and South polar regions

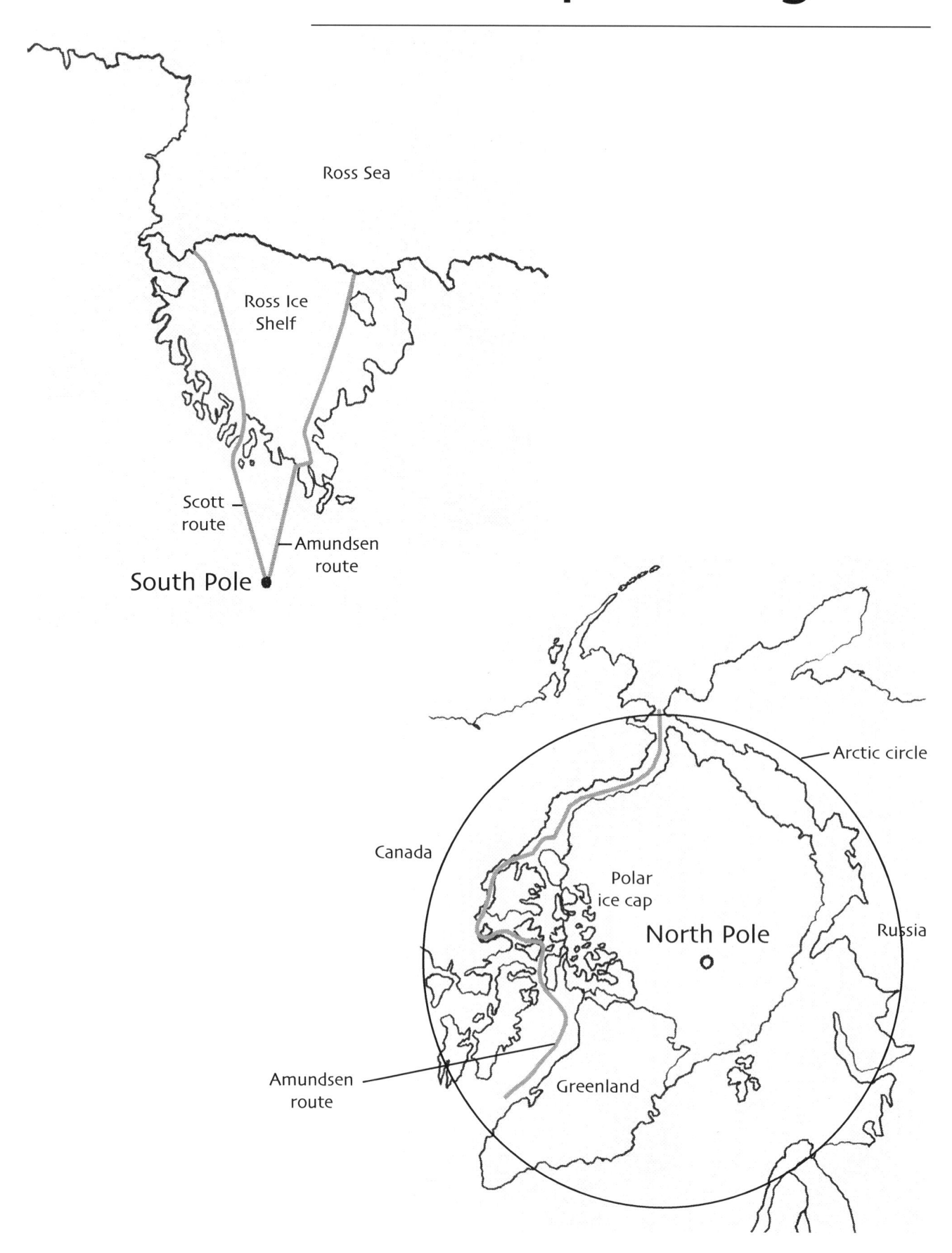

Ross Sea

Ross Ice Shelf

Scott route

Amundsen route

South Pole

Arctic circle

Canada

Polar ice cap

North Pole

Russia

Amundsen route

Greenland

38 CURRICULUM FOCUS • Famous journeys

Quotes from polar explorers

3 GENERIC SHEET

So we arrived and planted our flags. Thanks be to God. *Roald Amundsen*

Adventure is just bad planning. *Roald Amundsen*

We must always remember with gratitude and admiration the first sailors who steered their vessels through storms and mists and increased our knowledge of the land of ice in the south. *Roald Amundsen*

The English have loudly and openly told the world that skis and dogs are unusable in these regions and that fur clothes are rubbish. We will see... we will see... *Roald Amundsen.*

Great God, this is an awful place, and terrible enough for us to have laboured to it without the reward of priority. Well it is something to have got here, and the wind may be our friend tomorrow. We have turned our backs now on the goal of our ambition and must face 800 miles of solid dragging-and goodbye to most of the daydreams. *Robert Falcon Scott*

Better a live donkey than a dead lion. *Ernest Shackleton*

Superhuman effort isn't worth a damn unless it achieves results. *Ernest Shackleton*

Below the 40th latitude there is no law; below the 50th no God; below the 60th no common sense and below the 70th no intelligence whatsoever. *Kim Stanley Robinson.*

For skilled leadership give me Scott; for swift and efficient travel give me Amundsen; but when you are in a hopeless situation, when there seems to be no way out, get on your knees and pray for Shackleton. *Sir Raymond Priestly.*

We took risks. We knew we took them. Things have come out against us. We have no cause for complaint. *Robert Falcon Scott.*

I may say that this is the greatest factor-the way in which the expedition is equipped-the way in which every difficulty is foreseen and precautions taken for meeting and avoiding it. Victory awaits him who has everything in order; luck people call it. Defeat is certain for him who has neglected to take the necessary precautions in time; this is called bad luck. *Roald Amundsen.*

Beautiful weather for the last few days; the moon transforms the whole of this ice world into a fairyland. *Fridtjof Nansen*

Roald Amundsen questions and answers

4 GENERIC SHEET

When and where was Roald Amundsen born?

Roald Amundsen was born at Borge near the Norwegian capital city of Oslo on July 16th, 1872.

What did his mother want him to become?

Although all the family were mostly shipowners and sailors, Roald's mother wanted him to become a doctor.

What did Roald decide to do?

He went to university to train as a doctor. When his mother died, when he was twenty-one, Roald immediately left his studies and joined the Royal Norwegian Navy where he became interested in science.

Who were Amundsen's heroes?

The two men who most influenced what he wanted to do in life were the British sailor Sir John Franklin and the Norwegian explorer Fridtjof Nansen. Franklin died while trying to find the North West Passage while Nansen travelled extensively within the Arctic Circle.

Where did Amundsen go on his first expedition?

Between 1897 and 1899, Amundsen was first mate on a ship called the Belgica, which was commanded by Adrien de Gerlache. It became the first ship to spend a winter locked in the ice around Antarctica.

What did Amundsen achieve in 1903?

He successfully found the North West Passage linking the Atlantic and Pacific Oceans. With six others he travelled in a seal-hunting vessel called the Gjoa. They went via Baffin Bay, Lancaster and Peel Sounds and the James Ross, Simpson and Rae Straits. They stayed on King William Island and then travelled into the Beaufort Sea, through the Bering Strait between Russian and Alaska and into the Pacific.

What did Amundsen learn from the people of King William Island?

Amundsen learnt how to manage dog teams on long journeys over snow and also the benefits of wearing animal skins to keep warm in the very cold climate.

Why, in 1910, did Amundsen suddenly switch his interest to the South Pole?

He heard that other explorers, like the American Robert Peary, may have reached the North Pole already.

Who was also trying to reach the South Pole at that time?

Amundsen knew the Englishman, Robert Falcon Scott was trying to get to the South Pole around the same time and he wanted to beat him to it.

What was Amundsen's ship called and who had used it previously?

Amundsen sailed south in a ship called Fram. The word means forward in Norwegian. It has previously been used by Nansen, one of Amundsen's heroes.

Where did the Fram stop on the voyage south?

The Fram stopped at the Atlantic island of Madeira where they took on fresh water and other supplies. It was not until they left the island that Amundsen told most of the crew that they were heading for Antarctica and the South Pole.

Where did the party set up their base camp in Antarctica?

The Fram arrived at the edge of the Ross Ice Shelf on the western side of Antarctica on January 14th, 1911 and this is where the base camp was established. They called the base camp Framheim meaning the home of the Fram.

What held up the party for two months?

Food depots were set up initially and then, on April 21st, the sun went down for the long winter night. By late August the sun re-appeared but then they were held up by a spell of bad weather.

Why did Amundsen's party turn back on the final attempt to reach the South Pole?

They finally set out on September 11th but within a few days temperatures had gone down to – 50 degrees Celsius. They

CURRICULUM FOCUS • Famous journeys

could not find their way because compasses had become frozen so they were forced to head back to base camp.

When did the party finally reach the South Pole?

On mid-afternoon on Friday December 14th they reached the South Pole (90° 00' S). There were five men in the party. In addition to Amundsen they were Loav Bjaaland, Helmer Hanssen, Sverre Hassel and Oscar Wisting. They used sledges to carry their equipment pulled by teams of dogs. They celebrated with a meal of seal meat.

How did they check their position?

For several days they checked their location from the position of the Sun in the sky. They took readings from numerous points around the Pole to make sure they were correct.

What evidence did they leave behind at the Pole?

They erected a small tent proudly flying the Norwegian flag from its pole. Inside the tent they left a message for Scott and his party and in addition a letter to the ruler of Norway, King Haakon.

How long did the return journey take Amundsen?

It took thirty-nine days to make the return journey to base camp. The five men all got back safely and eleven of the remaining dogs. It was not until March 7th when they arrived in Tasmania that the news was announced.

How much later did Scott's group arrive at the South Pole?

Scott's group arrived at the South Pole thirty-five days after the Amundsen party. Scott's group, which included Edward Wilson, Henry Bowers, Edgar Evans and Laurence Oates, did not survive the return journey.

What book did Amundsen write about his experiences?

The story of Amundsen's experiences is told in the book The South Pole: an account of the Norwegian Antarctic Expedition in the Fram 1911-1912. It was published in 1912.

What other methods of transport did Amundsen become interested in?

Perhaps, because he was fed up with ice and snow preventing travel in the Arctic Circle, he began to take an interest in the development of manned flight. He obtained his pilot's licence and was now able to travel long distances quickly. It also meant the polar regions could be mapped more accurately.

What did Amundsen attempt to do in 1923?

He attempted to fly across the North Pole from Wainwright in Alaska to the island of Spitsbergen. The aircraft being used was damaged in flight and the journey had to be abandoned.

What flight did he take part in during 1925?

This time, with American engineer Lincoln Ellsworth, a pilot and two others, Amundsen took two Dornier flying boats to 87° 44' N, the furthest north an aircraft had reached at that time. When one of the aircraft was damaged, the group had to make an airstrip on the ice in order for the other one to take off with all of them aboard and reach safety.

Which airship did Amundsen use in 1926?

In 1926 Amundsen and a group of others, including Ellsworth and aeronautical engineer Umberto Nobile, made the first crossing of the Arctic in an airship. The craft was called Norge meaning Norway, Amundsen's homeland. Norwegian, Italian and American flags were dropped as the airship passed over the North Pole.

What record might Amundsen been able to claim?

If Peary had not been successful, Amundsen and his colleague Oscar Wisting might claim to be the first persons to reach both geographical poles, by land or air.

When did Amundsen set out on his last flight?

His last flight was made on June 11th, 1928.

What was he flying in?

With five other men he was flying in a French built Latham 47 seaplane.

What were they trying to do?

They were looking for Nobile's new airship, the Italia, which had reportedly crashed while returning from a flight to the North Pole.

Where did Amundsen's aircraft disappear?

It is believed the seaplane disappeared between Bear Island and Tromso on the Norwegian coast.

What seems to be the most likely cause of its disappearance?

It seems most likely that the seaplane crashed into the Barents Sea in thick fog. Later a wing float and a fuel tank from the aircraft was found but there was no sign of the six men. Both in 2004 and 2009 further searches under the sea were made by the Royal Norwegian Navy but there were no positive results.

Intrepid explorer

LESSON PLAN 1

History objectives
- To find out who Roald Amundsen was.
- To find out how he became a famous explorer.

Resources

- Large pictures, photographs of Roald Amundsen
- World maps showing the polar regions
- Pictures of the scenery and wildlife found in both the North and South Poles
- Map of Europe showing Scandinavia
- Class timeline
- Activity sheet 1-3
- Generic sheets 1-6

Starting points: whole class

Tell children they are going to find out about a famous person who devoted his life to exploring some of the most treacherous and most lonely places on the Earth. Explain that Roald Amundsen was anxious to find out as much as he could about travelling at both the North and South Poles. During his lifetime he managed to explore successfully across the sea, over the land and in the air.

Show children pictures of Amundsen and tell them he came from one of the countries in Scandinavia called Norway where people are more used to coping with snow and ice in the winter. Point out where Norway is on a map of Europe and its proximity to the Arctic Circle.

Talk about the major differences between the North and South Poles. Use enlarged versions of maps to aid the explanation. They are both very cold places but stress that basically the Arctic is a frozen ocean surrounded by land while the Antarctic is a frozen land surrounded by ocean.

Display a large map of the Arctic Circle and explain to children how, for many centuries, explorers had tried to find the North West Passage-a route linking the Atlantic and Pacific Oceans at the top of the world. Using the information given in the questions and answers on Generic sheet 4 plot the route that Amundsen and his colleagues followed in the ship called Gjoa.

Then explain how Amundsen switched his attention to Antarctica in an effort to become the first person to reach the South Pole. On a world map plot his journey from Norway to the Antarctic via the island of Madeira in the Atlantic Ocean aboard his new ship called the Fram. Pictures of Fram are shown on Generic sheet 1. Explain how he reached the South Pole first but do not go into detail as this famous trek will feature in Lesson 2.

Switch finally to examine the flight that Amundsen made over the North Pole with Umberto Nobile in the airship Norge. Use the information in the question and answer section on Generic sheet 5 and the pictures shown on Generic sheet 2. Plot the route followed on a map from Spitsbergen, Norway to Alaska. This was at the time when Amundsen became very interested in flight and realised that long distances over the Arctic could be more easily explored in an aircraft. Also, that the use of the aircraft was the best way of mapping these regions.

Stress that Amundsen explored across the area, over the land and in the air. Make a record of his main achievements on the class timeline. Journey through the North West Passage (1903-1905), Trek to the South Pole (1911-1912), Norge flight over the North Pole (1926).

Group activities

Activity sheet 1
On this activity sheet, children should study the pictures showing Amundsen's three main achievements. Stress the fact they include sea, land and air travel. The missing words should be filled in to complete the short sentences under the pictures. Some help may be needed with the spelling of the words. Provide a word bank, if necessary.

Activity sheet 2
The same three pictures are provided on this activity sheet but here children are required to write their own captions. Key words are provided for them at the bottom of the sheet.

Activity sheet 3
More able children are provided with just pictures on this worksheet and are required to write as full a description as possible about each event. It may be necessary to talk about the events co-operatively in pairs or small groups first so children are clear about what the pictures show. Again, it may be helpful to provide some key words or assist children with accurate spelling especially concerning the names of places. Provide extra paper for the children's writing.

Plenary session

Revise the three main events in Amundsen's life that have been featured on the activity sheets. Emphasise again how Amundsen was prepared to use sea, land and air transport as a way of extending the scope of his exploration.

- Which do children consider the most dangerous way to explore in polar regions, by sea, land or air? Ask them to give reasons.
- Which method would they prefer to use and why?
- What do they consider to be Amundsen's greatest exploration achievement?
- Given a choice, would children prefer to explore the ice-bound waters in the Arctic or the frozen wastes of the Antarctic?

Ideas for support

Finding and reading information about geographical locations is an essential element involved in this lesson. It is important therefore that a varied selection of good quality maps are available for use throughout. Display them around the classroom so children get used to seeing them and the information they contain. Globes may also be useful to help pinpoint the positions of both the North and South Pole. Also provide support plotting the routes of Amundsen's journeys and, if possible, calculating approximate distances using a scale.

Ideas for extension

Encourage children to research the lives and achievements of other notable polar explorers who all helped to extend our knowledge of these lonely and difficult places. Start with Amundsen's particular heroes like Sir John Franklin and Fridtjof Nansen and move on to others like Henry Hudson, John Davis, Martin Frobisher, Willem Barents, John Ross, Robert Peary, Ernest Shackleton and Robert Falcon Scott.

- Which particular locations did they explore in?
- Which famous ships are associated with their journeys?
- Which explorers survived their journeys and lived to tell the tale?
- Which explorers lost their lives or were never heard of again?

Intrepid Explorer

Name ....

Here are pictures of Roald Amundsen's three main achievements.

Fill in the missing words to complete the sentences under each one.

Across the sea

The North West Page joined the _____

and _____ Oceans.

Over the land

Roald Amundsen from _____

beat Robert Scott from _____ to reach

the _____ first.

In the air

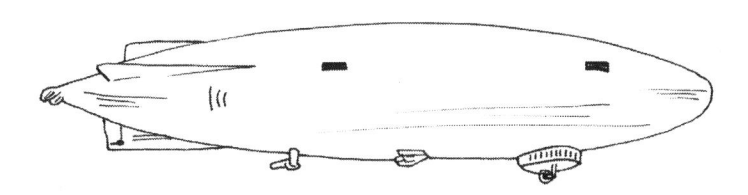

The airship _____ crossed the North Pole from

_____ to _____

ACTIVITY SHEET 2

Intrepid Explorer

Name ....

Here are pictures of Roald Amundsen's three greatest achievements

Write a sentence to describe what is happening in each picture. A word bank is provided at the bottom of the sheet to help you

Across the sea

_____

_____

Over the land

_____

_____

In the air

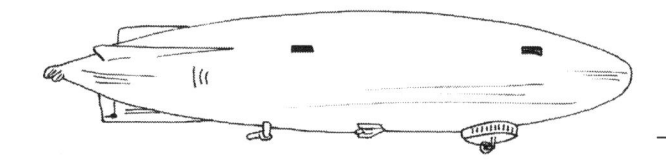

_____

_____

Word bank
North West Passage Atlantic Pacific Oceans South Pole North Pole Robert Falcon Scott Norge airship Umberto Nobile sailed flew walked dog team flight

46   CURRICULUM FOCUS • Famous journeys

Intrepid Explorer

3 ACTIVITY SHEET

Name ....

Here are pictures of Roald Amundsen's three greatest achievements.

Write in as much detail as possible a description of each event.

Across the sea

Finding the North West Passage (1903-1905)

_____

_____

_____

Over the land

Reaching the South Pole (1911-1912)

_____

_____

_____

In the air

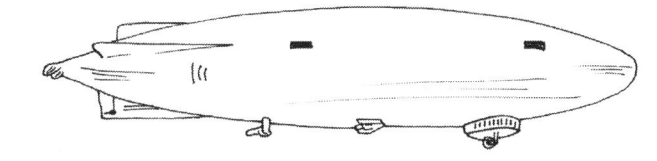

Flight over the North Pole (1926)

_____

_____

_____

CURRICULUM FOCUS • Famous journeys 47

LESSON PLAN 2: The race to the South Pole

History objectives
- To find out about the race to get to the South Pole first.
- To understand how we know what happened during this race.

Resources

- Activity sheets 1-3
- Generic sheet 1-6
- Large display map of Antarctica
- Range of coloured pencils/pens
- If possible, extracts from Amundsen's account of the journey to the South Pole and Scott's diary of his unsuccessful journey.

Starting points: whole class

Compare and contrast the voyages Amundsen and Scott made to get to the South Pole. Amundsen travelled from Norway aboard the Fram, stopping at Madeira to take on fresh supplies. Scott sailed from Cardiff in the Terra Nova and called in at Australia and New Zealand before making landfall on Antarctica.

Also look at the locations where the two men made their base camps when they arrived in Antarctica. Amundsen set up camp at a place he called Framheim (home of the Fram) on the part of the Ross Ice Shelf known as The Bay of Whales. During the winter of 1911, Scott's party made a hut at Cape Evans on Ross Island their home. Show the locations of both camps on the large map of Antarctica. Amundsen's route to the South Pole was 90 kilometres shorter than the one used by Scott.

Compare the type of equipment used by both the explorers as they tried to reach the South Pole. Amundsen's group used only dog teams throughout the whole journey while Scott started out with dogs, horses and two motorised sledges that soon broke down. Later the horses became exhausted and the dogs returned when the group set out for the final part of the journey. Scott's men wore largely woollen outfits while Amundsen favoured sealskin and fur, something he had learned from the Inuit people of the Arctic Circle.

Consider the make-up of the two groups heading for the South Pole. Amundsen's party consisted of Amundsen, Olav Bjaaland, Helmer Hanssen, Sverre Hassel and Oscar Wisting. They were all expert skiers and dog handlers and often covered 40 kilometres per day. Scott's group was made up of Laurence Oates, Edgar Evans, Henry Bowers and Edward Wilson. They pulled their own sledge.

Discuss the reactions of the two parties when they finally reached the South Pole, Amundsen on December 14th, 1911 and Scott on January 16th, 1912. Amundsen wrote, 'The atmosphere in the tent is like the eve of some great festival.' Scott wrote, 'It is a terrible disappointment and I am very sorry for my loyal companions.'

Talk about what happened on the return journey. Amundsen's group completed the trek back in thirty-nine days. All five men were in good spirits and eleven of the dogs survived the journey. Of Scott's group, Evans died soon after leaving the South Pole. Oates died later and finally Scott, Bowers and Wilson died together in the tent during bad storms.

Tell children we know so much about what happened on the journeys to the South Pole because both explorers wrote personal and detailed records of what happened to them. Amundsen wrote a book about the expedition that was published in 1912 while Scott kept a diary of each day's events during the trek to the Pole. In history, these are called primary sources. Scott's diary was recovered when his body was found some eight months after he had died.

Finally encourage children to think about the reasons why Amundsen's journey to reach and return from the South Pole was successful and why Scott's was not. Consider factors like earlier start time, length of journey, methods of transport, type of clothing, better weather conditions etc.

Group activities

Activity sheet 1
The map on this activity sheet shows the continent of Antarctica. Children are required to mark on the different routes followed by the two explorers Roald Amundsen and Robert Falcon Scott from the base camps to the South Pole. Provide different coloured pens for children to use. Encourage discussion about the different starting places and the journey the explorers took.

Activity sheet 2
Routes should also be marked with different coloured pens on this activity sheet. Under the map children are asked to write a short diary extract giving Amundsen's reaction when he first reached the South Pole on December 14th, 1911. Discuss with children first how he might have felt and what would be the best way to celebrate the achievement.

Activity sheet 3
This activity sheet, for more able children, also contains the same map of Antarctica. Once the routes have been marked on the map, encourage children to think about the contrasting feelings of the two explorers when they reached the South Pole. Amundsen knew he was first so would have been jubilant while Scott would experience all the disappointment of being 'pipped at the post'. These feelings should be reflected in the diary entries children write at the bottom of the sheet.

Plenary

Review in more detail, the similarities and differences between the approaches taken by the two explorers. Amundsen used dogs for the whole journey, for example, started first and decided on a shorter route. Scott travelled further, knew Amundsen was probably ahead of him and only relied on manpower to pull sledges. In a role-play situation, children could be chosen to act the parts of Amundsen and Scott while others could put questions to them. Why did you decide not to use/ to use dogs? What type of clothing were you wearing? What was the hardest part of the journey? How did it feel to reach the South Pole?

Ideas for support

Provide assistance with map work so that the routes of both Amundsen and Scott are plotted carefully. Give support also on the method of writing concise diary entries so that children focus on the important points they want to make. If possible, read them examples from Amundsen's book and Scott's diary. Also look at the quotations on Generic page 3 which give the flavour of how explorers have considered carrying out expeditions in the polar regions.

Ideas for extension

Focus on the major differences between the Arctic and Antarctic. The Arctic Ocean is about five times larger than the Mediterranean Sea with drifting ice some 30 metres thick. Polar bears, foxes and reindeer are among the creatures that can live in Arctic conditions. Seals, walruses and fish live in the seas and people have established settlements well within the Arctic Circle. The Antarctic, on the other hand, covers one tenth of the Earth's surface and is covered with sheet ice 4500 metres thick. There are high mountains and the only people who live there are scientists and researchers. There are no land animals although the vast Southern Ocean does support whales, seals, penguins and many species of gull.

ACTIVITY SHEET 1

The race to the South Pole

Name ....

This map shows the continent of Antarctica. Show the locations where Amundsen and Scott had their base camps.

Then show the different routes they followed to reach the South Pole.

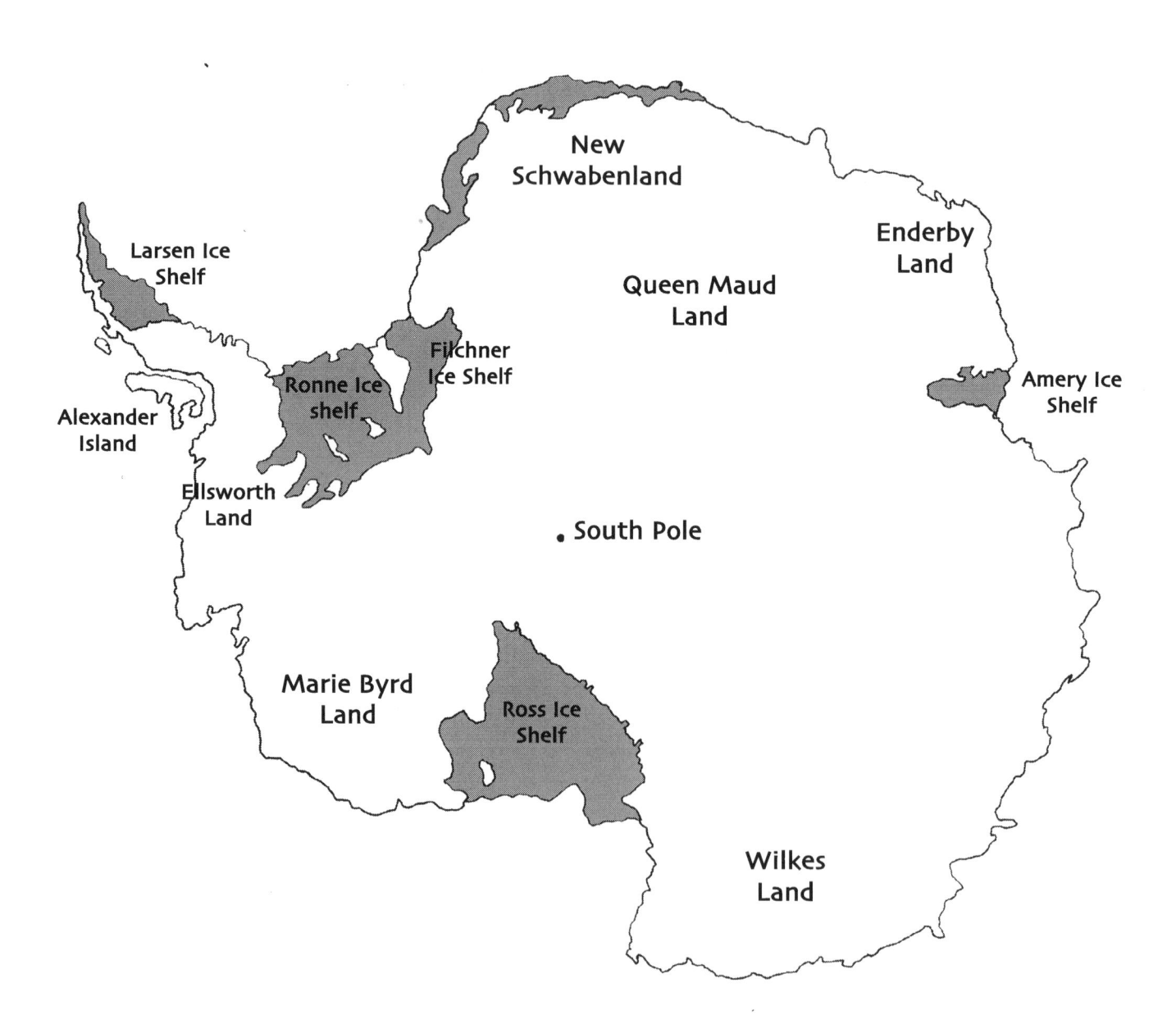

- Larsen Ice Shelf
- New Schwabenland
- Enderby Land
- Queen Maud Land
- Filchner Ice Shelf
- Ronne Ice shelf
- Amery Ice Shelf
- Alexander Island
- Ellsworth Land
- South Pole
- Marie Byrd Land
- Ross Ice Shelf
- Wilkes Land

50 CURRICULUM FOCUS • Famous journeys

The race to the South Pole

ACTIVITY SHEET 2

Name ....

This map shows the continent of Antarctica. Show the locations where Amundsen and Scott had their base camps. Then show the different routes they followed to reach the South Pole.

Under the map, write down what you think Amundsen might have written in his diary on the day he first reached the South Pole.

Diary entry

December 14th, 1911

_____
_____
_____
_____
_____
_____
_____
_____

CURRICULUM FOCUS • Famous journeys

ACTIVITY SHEET 3

The race to the South Pole

Name ....

This map shows the continent of Antarctica. Show the locations where Amundsen and Scott had their base camps. Then show the different routes they followed to reach the South Pole.

Map of Antarctica showing: New Schwabenland, Larsen Ice Shelf, Enderby Land, Queen Maud Land, Filchner Ice Shelf, Ronne Ice shelf, Amery Ice Shelf, Alexander Island, Ellsworth Land, South Pole, Marie Byrd Land, Ross Ice Shelf, Wilkes Land.

Under the map write the diary entries for both Amundsen and Scott when they arrived at the South Pole. Show in your writing why their feelings would have been so different.

Diary entry

Amundsen: December 14th, 1911

_____

_____

_____

Scott: January 16th, 1912

_____

_____

_____

CURRICULUM FOCUS • Famous journeys

The scientific age

LESSON PLAN 3

History objectives
- To find out what life is like in Antarctica
- To find out how developments in science and technology has made living and working there easier.

Resources

- Activity sheets 1-3
- Pictures of the special kinds of machinery featured on the activity sheets as well as examples of people working in the Antarctic landscape.

Starting points: whole class

Explain to children that because the Earth is tilted, the amount of sun reaching the surface varies throughout the year. When the North Pole is tilted towards the sun, it is summer north of the equator. Six months later the Earth has done half its yearly journey around the sun, the North Pole is tilted away and it is winter in the north and summer in the south.

Tell them how polar exploration has changed. Say that in 1954 a different way was found to reach the North Pole. The United States Navy submarine Nautilus reached it by travelling under the Arctic sea-ice. Five years later the submarine Skate went one better. It used its radar to find a weak spot in the ice near the pole and then surfaced as close to this position as it could get.

Talk about the fact that unlike the Arctic, Antarctica has no native people living there. It is only home to the scientists, technicians and researchers who carry out work there during the summer months. Through the summer they go out each day to study the rocks, glaciers, snow and ice. Through the dark winter months though only a few essential workers remain and the Antarctic is almost deserted.

Recap on the type of equipment used by Amundsen and Scott at the beginning of the twentieth century when manpower was often key. Then look at pictures of the equipment they use in Antarctica now to travel around and carry out research. Focus on the 'then and now' aspect of the changes and explain how developments in science and technology have made life much easier. Show children pictures of methods of transport like the Hercules C-130 supply plane, light aircraft fitted with skis, ice-breaking ships, caterpillar tractors, skidoos etc.

Talk about some of the research that is carried out. Think about arrays of radar aerials that allow scientists to study space above the South Pole. Hydrogen filled weather balloons, tracked by radar, allow meteorologists to study winds and other aspects of the weather including climate change. Doctors study how the human body reacts to cold, long periods without daylight and changes in diet.

Activity sheet 1
This sheet is intended for children who will need support to recognise visual information about the type of equipment used in Antarctica these days. They are required to match the items of equipment shown in the pictures with captions. It may be necessary to discuss the pictures with them first.

Activity sheet 2
In this activity children have to write a short descriptive sentence about each of the pieces of equipment shown in the pictures. A word bank is provided to help them with vocabulary and spelling but some discussion of the pictures will also be needed.

Activity sheet 3
On this activity sheet for more able pupils, children are required to give full detailed descriptions of each of the pieces of equipment shown. Stress that children should focus not only on what the items are but also what activities they are able to carry out and how this might be useful to the scientists and researchers working in an environment like the Antarctic.

Plenary

Recap on the pieces of writing that children have produced. Read out some of the descriptions they have used and talk about the functions the items of equipment carry out. How are they specially adapted to suit the harsh climate of Antarctica? How do they help scientists carry out their work? How would scientists manage without them? Why do operations have to stop during the Antarctic winter?

Ideas for support

Plenty of visual resources will be needed if children are to derive maximum benefit from these activities. Set up displays in the classroom so children can look at various machines in detail. Focus also on how the equipment used has been adapted for working in a cold climate and how many of the tasks scientists do could not easily be carried out safely without the help of these devices.

Ideas for extension

Encourage children to think about the kind of scientific studies they would like to carry out in Antarctica. What equipment would they need? Find out more about the type of clothing they would need to wear. It will need to be light and flexible so they can move around easily but still warm enough to keep out snowstorms, biting winds and hard frosts, Challenge them to draw a plan of the layout of the inside of a science station near the South Pole. They should include kitchens, sleeping accommodation, leisure areas including a gym, a communications room etc. Underground tunnels link some bases so people do not need to go outside during severe blizzards.

The scientific age

Name ....

Look at these pictures of the equipment that is used today exploring Antarctica.

Cut out the pictures and the captions below and match them up.

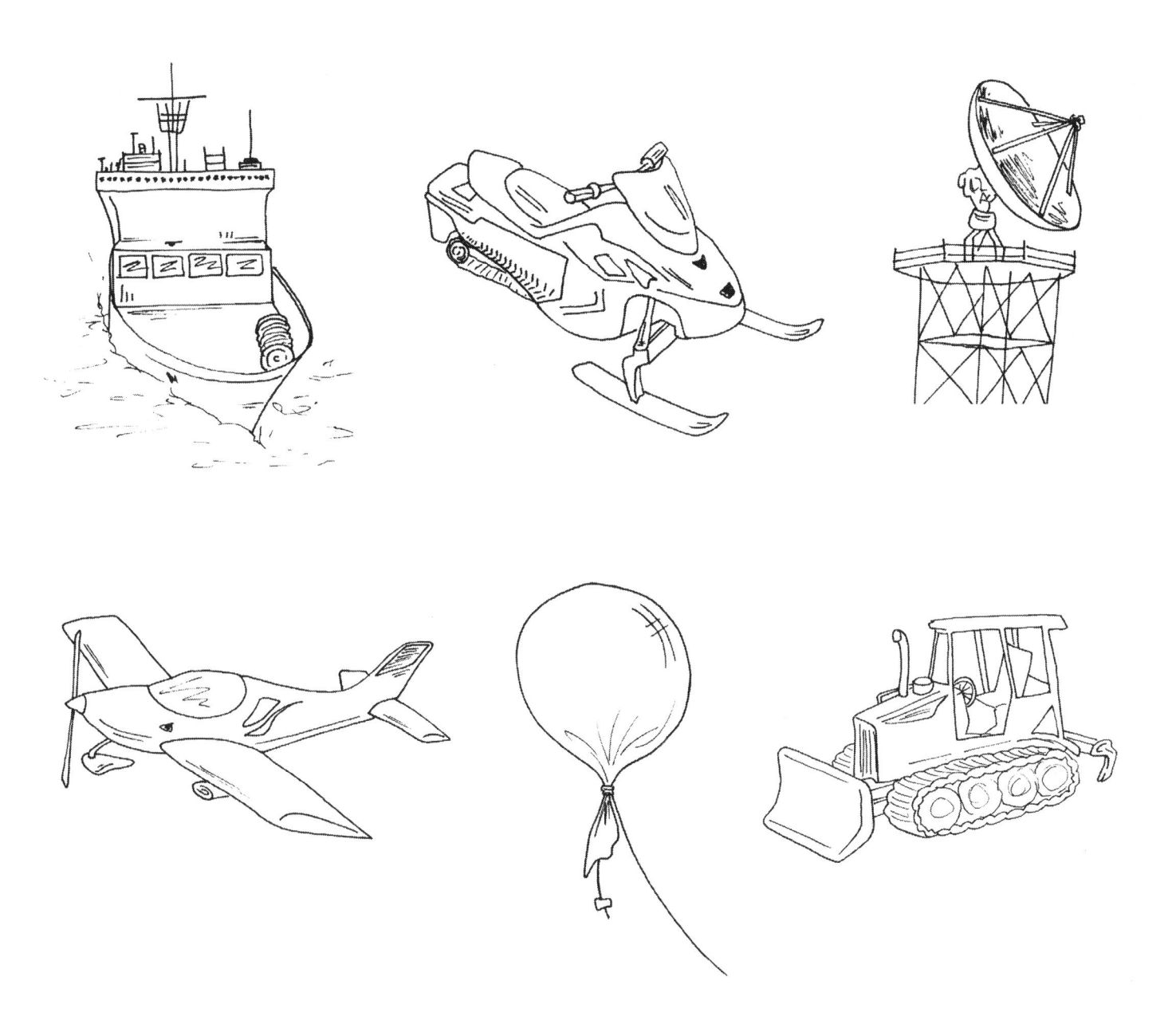

| skidoo | light aircraft | caterpillar tractor | radar |
| weather balloon | ice breaking ship |

CURRICULUM FOCUS • Famous journeys 55

ACTIVITY SHEET 2

The scientific age

Name ....

Here are some pictures of the equipment used today exploring Antarctica.

Write a sentence about how each one is used. Use the word bank at the bottom of the sheet to help you.

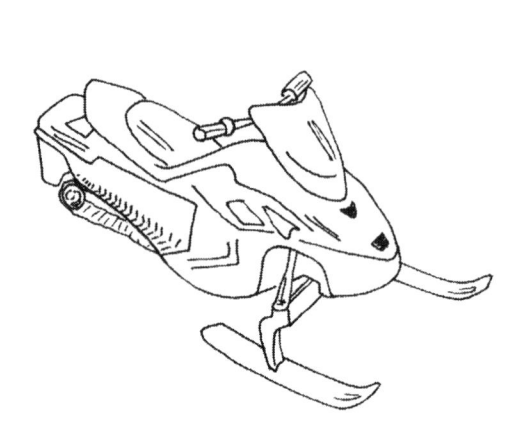

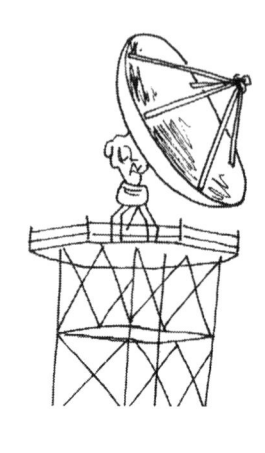

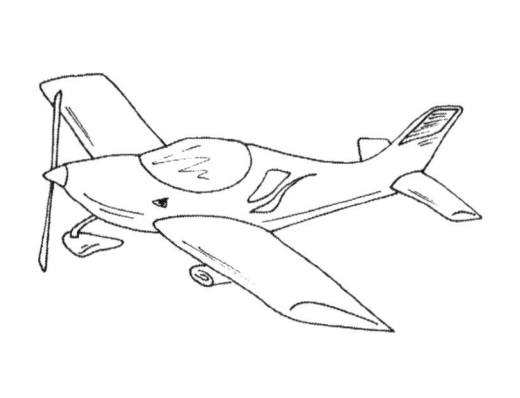

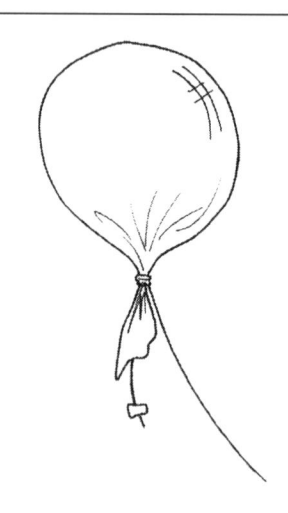

_____   _____   _____
_____   _____   _____

_____   _____   _____
_____   _____   _____

Word bank
aircraft tractor skis propellers motor toboggan hydrogen ice breaker bows
snow ice shovel frozen hull weather data meteorology

56 CURRICULUM FOCUS · Famous journeys

The scientific age

Name ....

Here are some pictures of the equipment that is used exploring Antarctica today.

Find out more about each item of equipment and write about it underneath the correct picture.

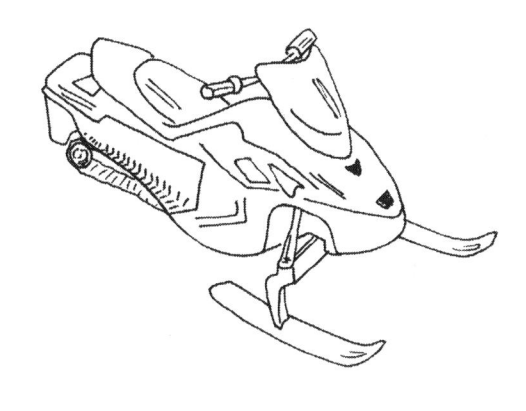

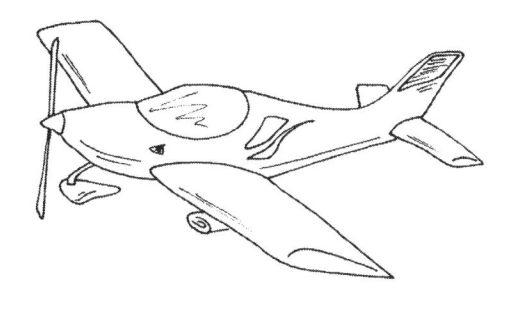

CURRICULUM FOCUS • Famous journeys 57

Neil Armstrong

TEACHERS' NOTES

Famous words

In July 1969 Neil Armstrong uttered some of the most quoted words in the history of the world. When his spacecraft landed on the Moon he told listeners on Earth, 'The Eagle has landed'. Later, as he moved down onto the lunar surface, 'That's one small step for (a) man, one giant leap for mankind,' sounded out through space.

Armstrong had made the journey to the Moon aboard Apollo 11 and in the company of Edwin 'Buzz' Aldrin and Michael Collins. Armstrong and Aldrin were selected to travel down to the Moon's surface in the Lunar Module while Collins continued to orbit around the Moon in the Service Module. For two hours Armstrong and Aldrin explored and investigated the surface of the Moon before being re-united with Collins for the return journey to Earth. All this was watched on television by over five hundred million people-a fifth of the world's total population. After eight days in space, the astronauts returned safely to Earth where, for Armstrong and his companions, life would never really be the same again.

Early flight

Neil Armstrong developed a fascination for flying from a very early age. Born in 1930, he was brought up in the American state of Ohio where his father, an accountant, moved around from town to town monitoring local council finances. One of these locations, Cleveland, had its own airport and it was here that Armstrong, aged only two, started to watch the aeroplanes flying in and out.

By the age of six the young Armstrong had been on his first flight. Father and son sneaked off church one Sunday to see a plane nicknamed 'The Tin Goose' at Warren Airport and, after getting into conversation with the pilot, were offered a short ride. Neil was hooked and very soon he was spending all his spare time assembling model aircraft. He was able to read early and among the aviation pioneers he found out about were the Wright Brothers who had worked on their first aircraft not far from the farm where Neil's grandparents still lived.

The love affair with aeroplanes continued and when Armstrong became a teenager he was soon earning as much as possible so that he could finance flying lessons. Initially he had to work for over twenty hours to pay for a single lesson but the long hours do not deter him. He was soon able to afford his first flying lesson and by the age of sixteen he had qualified for his student pilot's licence.

When he left school Neil Armstrong was anxious to follow up his interest in aeronautics, the science of flight, at university. His education was paid for by a Navy scholarship and in 1947 he started a course of aeronautical engineering at Purdue University in Indiana. Soon after he began his university studies however a war broke out in Korea, a small country close to China in Asia. The United States Navy wanted skilful young pilots and in 1950, at the age of 19, Neil Armstrong became a fighter pilot. After rapid training he was assigned to the aircraft carrier, the USS Essex. Armstrong flew over 70 missions in the Korean War, often having to fly very low at high speeds and to show split-second reactions. There were several near misses and on one occasion his plan crashed and exploded shortly after he had managed to parachute to safety. He was awarded medals for his bravery and in 1952, his tour of duty over, he returned to university to complete his studies.

Test pilot

After a short spell working at the Lewis Flight Propulsion Laboratory in Cleveland, Ohio, Armstrong landed the job he had been seeking since leaving university. He joined the staff at Edwards Air Force Base, California where the National Aeronautics and Space Administration (NASA) were carrying out some interesting tests. Armstrong's own personal 'space age' was about to begin.

At Edwards Air Force Base, Armstrong worked as a test pilot. Some flights checked on how high an aircraft could fly while others assessed its speed or manoeuvrability. In another series of tests, pilots like Armstrong took a full-sized model of a space capsule to 21000 metres and from there they tried different types of parachutes in a series of test drops. Neil Armstrong also became one of the few pilots to fly the X-15, a sleek, winged rocket plane which would drop from a Boeing B-52 'mother' aircraft, travel to the edge of the atmosphere and then glide back to Earth without power. It reached over 60000 metres, almost six times higher than the height at which modern jet aircraft travel.

Into 'The Nine'

Armstrong might well have continued piloting more planes to the edge of space but in 1962 NASA's main goal changed. It was to abandon sending rocket planes to the limits of the atmosphere and concentrate instead on putting a man on the Moon. 'Space is the frontier and that's where I intend to go,' said Neil Armstrong. By September of that year he had become a member of 'The Nine', as one of the first groups of NASA astronauts were called. Armstrong and other members of the group trained for missions in two-man space capsules, given the name Gemini-the twins. These capsules were intended to orbit the Earth and prepare for eventual lunar flights. There were many different

CURRICULUM FOCUS • Famous journeys

routines to learn and practise. These included experiencing high-speed flight and weightlessness as well as docking procedures where pieces of space equipment linked together. Other flights stayed in space for as long as possible to test the astronauts' powers of endurance. In August 1965, Armstrong was selected as back-up crew for Gemini 5. He remained on Earth as astronauts Gordon Cooper and Pete Conrad set a new record by orbiting the Earth for eight days. The hard work done by Neil Armstrong during this mission, however, had put him in a good position and, seven months later, his chance was to come on Gemini 8.

The Gemini Mission

It was on March 16th, 1966 that Neil Armstrong and his co-pilot, David Scott, took off on Gemini 8. The main purpose of the mission was to 'dock' or join together with an orbiting satellite. This routine had never been carried out before. The two astronauts would have to position the Gemini spacecraft correctly in order to meet with the satellite before joining the two together in space. The 'docking' itself was not a problem but, once joined, the two spacecraft, 300 kilometres above the Earth, began to spin wildly out of control. Even when Armstrong successfully separated the two craft, the Gemini capsule continued to spin. He quickly realised that one of the steering motors had stuck open and he was forced to use one of the re-entry thrusters to steady the craft. The use of these thrusters meant the mission had to be aborted and, after only ten hours in space, Gemini 8 was forced to return to Earth. NASA officials had been impressed with Armstrong's quick thinking and steady nerves and these were qualities they would consider carefully when selecting crew for a mission to the Moon.

Getting ready

The Apollo missions that were to land a man on the Moon did not start successfully. The three astronauts from Apollo 1 died in a fire on the ground during testing in 1969 and the following year Neil Armstrong was involved in a serious accident himself. He was testing an LLRV (Lunar Landing Research Vehicle) 30 metres in the air when it started to tilt over to one side. As it went further out of control Armstrong ejected to safety by using his parachute. He landed without injury while the vehicle crashed to the ground and exploded.

Armstrong stood by as back-up crew for Apollo 8 before, in January 1969, being assigned to Apollo 11. Edwin 'Buzz' Aldrin and Michael Collins were selected to be his fellow crew-members. Armstrong and Aldrin would travel down to the Moon's surface while Collins would remain in the 'mother' ship, the Service Module, orbiting around the Moon. It was decided to call the Command Module Columbia in honour of an American song and the Lunar Module would be code-named Eagle, the symbol of the United States of America.

There followed an intensive period of training. The three crewmen often spent fourteen hours a day practising their routines in simulators, models or imitations of the real craft they would be using. There were hours of discussion and medical tests as well as lectures on space travel and rocketry, the stars and planets within the Solar System and the geology of the Moon. The astronauts were putting their faith in an array of state-of-the-art technology. The three-stage Saturn 5 rocket would take them into space. This, along with other sections, would be jettisoned along the way. Only the Command Module would finally make it back to Earth.

Blast off

The history-making week in Neil Armstrong's life would begin on July 16th, 1969. One million people arrived at Cape Kennedy to witness the take-off with millions more glued to television screens at home. Armstrong was up soon after 4.00 a.m. and had breakfast. He was in his spacesuit by 6.00 o'clock. Soon a van called to take the three astronauts to the launch pad where the space rocket, complete with its attachments, reached up over one hundred metres into the sky. Just after 9.30 a.m. the Saturn's rockets burst into action and the mission had begun. Within two and a half minutes of take-off, the first rocket stage had fallen away and six minutes later the second stage followed in the same way. The spacecraft was now out of the atmosphere and moving into orbit over 180 kilometres above the Earth. Less than three hours after take-off, the third stage fired again pushing the spaceship away from the Earth and towards the Moon. After abandoning the third stage, the craft continued on its journey, rotating slowly at intervals so that no parts were exposed to the Sun for too long causing overheating. Meanwhile, on board cameras kept Mission Control in touch with what was going on and, all over the world, millions of people looked in on the routine activities carried out by Armstrong and other members of the crew.

Moon landing

Four days into the mission the crew were orbiting the Moon and Armstrong and Aldrin slid into the Lunar Module, Eagle, ready to begin the descent to the Moon's surface. Once the pair landed the intention was to sleep for several hours before venturing outside. Excitement, however, got the better of them and climbing into their special spacesuits they were ready to leave the Lunar Module by 9.30 p.m. Aldrin set the special television camera into operation so the astronauts could be filmed as they set foot on the Moon's surface. When they were ready Armstrong climbed carefully down the small ladder before speaking those famous words. 'That's one small step for (a) man, one giant leap for mankind.' A few minutes later Aldrin joined him and the pair set about carrying out their pre-arranged activities.

The two men were to spend less than two hours on the Moon's surface but there was a lot to do. They collected rock and dust samples, set up a series of scientific experiments and planted the American flag. The flag had a metal rod attached to hold it in a horizontal position, as there is no wind on the Moon. They also found time to speak directly to the President of the United States, Richard Nixon. All their exploits were watched on television by an estimated five hundred million people, about a fifth of the world's total population.

After a period of rest it was time to return to Columbia. The Eagle separated into two halves, one half remaining on the Moon, while the other section sped back towards Columbia where Michael Collins was patiently waiting. Three hours later the two parts docked, the operation Armstrong had practised three years earlier on his first space mission. With the three astronauts re-united, Eagle was allowed to fall back to the surface of the Moon while Columbia blasted off for its difficult journey back to Earth.

Safe return

With Earth approaching, the Service Module was also jettisoned and now only the dome-shaped Command Module was left to return the astronauts home. After nine days in space the three explorers splashed down into the Pacific Ocean about 1300 kilometres from the island of Hawaii. Soon helicopters arrived and transported the men and the capsule to the waiting USS Hornet. Once on board the aircraft-carrier, Armstrong, Aldrin and Collins went into a period of quarantine until August 10th while NSAS scientists made sure they had not brought back any contagious germs from the Moon. President Nixon was able to see the astronauts through a window and speak to them with the aid of a microphone when he visited them on the USS Hornet.

After the period spent in quarantine, the three astronauts were welcomed at ticker-tape welcomes in New York and Chicago. In the city of Los Angeles they were awarded the USA's highest civilian honour, the Presidential Medal of Freedom. Neil Armstrong was also presented with a number of other important medals but also found time to visit his hometown of Wapakoneta where thousands of people lined the route to cheer him. A world tour followed with the three astronauts visiting a total of twenty-eight cities in twenty-five countries.

After Apollo

Throughout his career Neil Armstrong had never been keen on publicity so following the world tour he did his best to avoid it. For several years he continued to work for NASA and he was then appointed Professor of Aerospace Engineering at the University of Cincinnati in his home state of Ohio. He bought a farm nearby and left the university in 1979. In 1986 he was appointed vice-chairman of the enquiry investigating the death of seven astronauts aboard the Space Shuttle Challenger that exploded soon after take-off. He has also served as chairman of a New York electronics company. A number of other honours have been bestowed on him over the years and there are schools and other public buildings named after him throughout America.

In many ways though, Armstrong has always been a private person who, unlike many other astronauts, has usually refused to make public appearances and feature in television programmes. It was not until 2005 that he worked on his first authorised biography, First Man: The Life of Neil A. Armstrong, which was written in collaboration with James R. Hansen. He has, in his memoirs, expressed his concerns about the Apollo 11 mission that he originally rated as having only a fifty-fifty chance of making it as far as the Moon landing. 'I was elated, ecstatic and extremely surprised that we were successful,' he said later. He continues to remain puzzled by all the publicity that he still gets for his moonwalk. For him it was the culmination of a vast team effort in which everyone involved should feel proud of their achievements.

Neil Armstrong

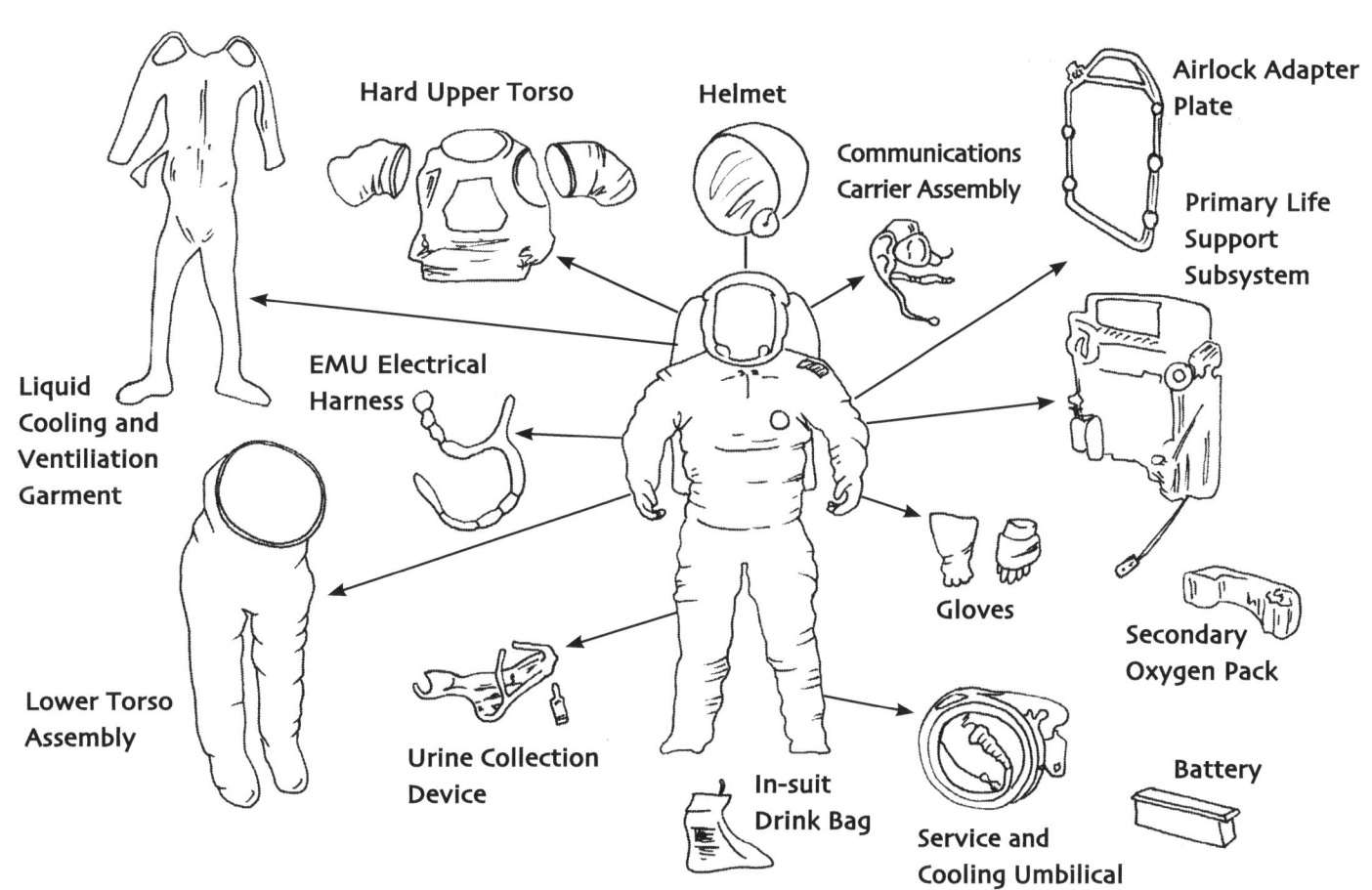

1 GENERIC SHEET

- Liquid Cooling and Ventiliation Garment
- Hard Upper Torso
- Helmet
- Communications Carrier Assembly
- Airlock Adapter Plate
- Primary Life Support Subsystem
- EMU Electrical Harness
- Lower Torso Assembly
- Urine Collection Device
- In-suit Drink Bag
- Gloves
- Service and Cooling Umbilical
- Secondary Oxygen Pack
- Battery

CURRICULUM FOCUS • Famous journeys 61

Timeline of the main events in Neil Armstrong's life

1930	• Born **August 5, 1930**
1940	• From **1949** to **1952**, Armstrong was a naval aviator
1950	• In **1955**, Neil Armstrong earned a bachelor's degree in aeronautical engineering from Purdue University. • He married Janet Elizabeth Shearon on **January 28, 1956.**
1960	• In 1962, he resolved to become an astronaut and became America's first non military astronaut in **September 1962**. • First spaceflight was aboard Gemini 8 in **1966** • Armstrong's second and last spaceflight was as mission commander of the Apollo 11 moon landing mission on **July 20, 1969**. • On **24th July 1969**, they returned to their mother Earth.
1970	• In **1970**, he was honoured with the Robert H. Goddard Memorial Trophy. • He resigned from NASA in **1971** and started working at the University of Cincinnati in Ohio.
1980	
1990	• Armstrong married Carol Knight on **June 12, 1994**. This was his second marriage.
2000	• Armstrong's authorized biography titled 'First Man: The Life of Neil A. Armstrong' was brought out in the year **2005**.

Saturn 5 Rocket

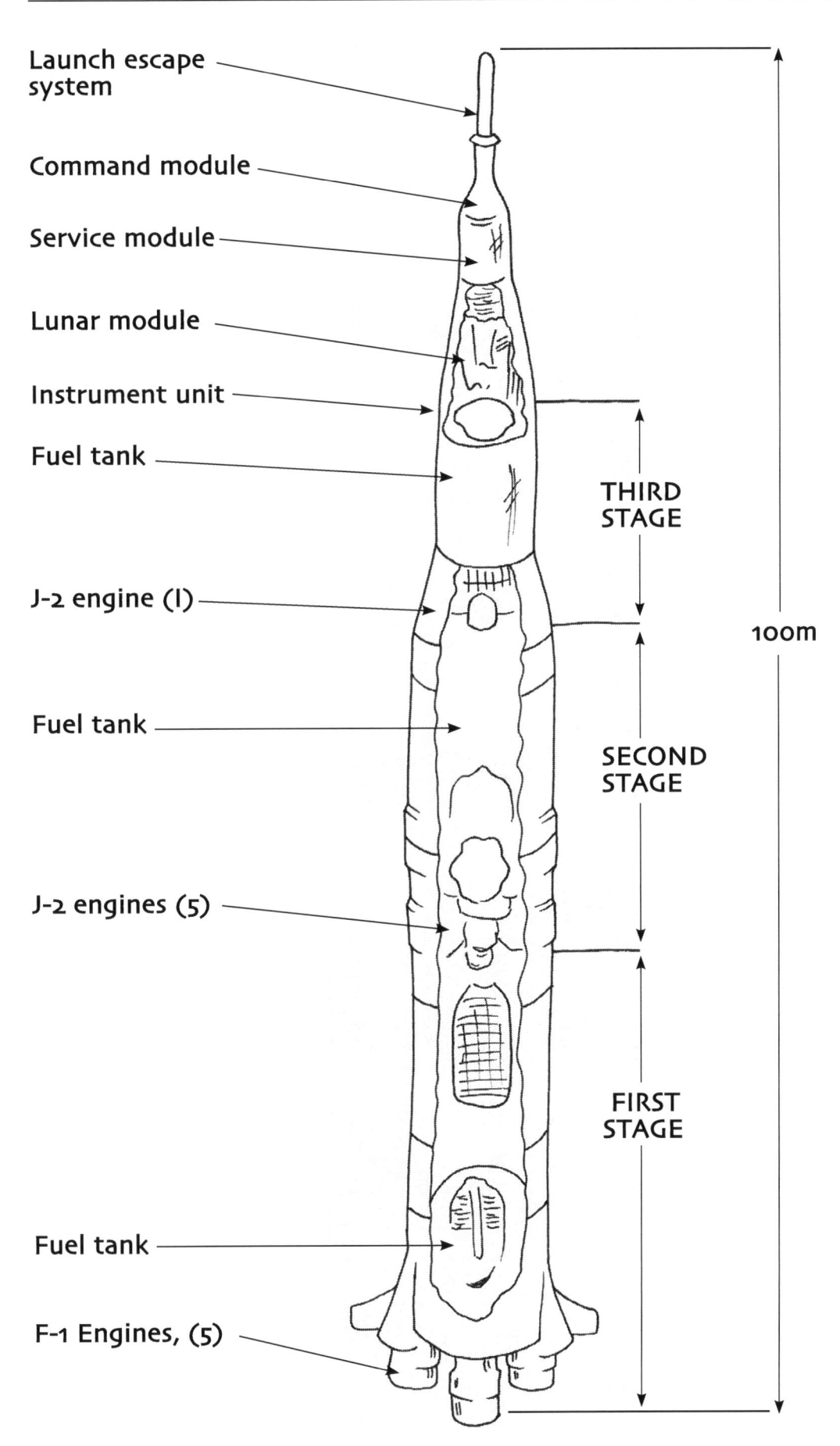

3 GENERIC SHEET

- Launch escape system
- Command module
- Service module
- Lunar module
- Instrument unit
- Fuel tank

THIRD STAGE

- J-2 engine (1)

- Fuel tank

SECOND STAGE

- J-2 engines (5)

FIRST STAGE

- Fuel tank
- F-1 Engines, (5)

100m

CURRICULUM FOCUS • Famous journeys 63

4 GENERIC SHEET

First step on the Moon

Capsule splashing down in the Pacific Ocean.

64 CURRICULUM FOCUS • Famous journeys

Phases in the Moon cycle

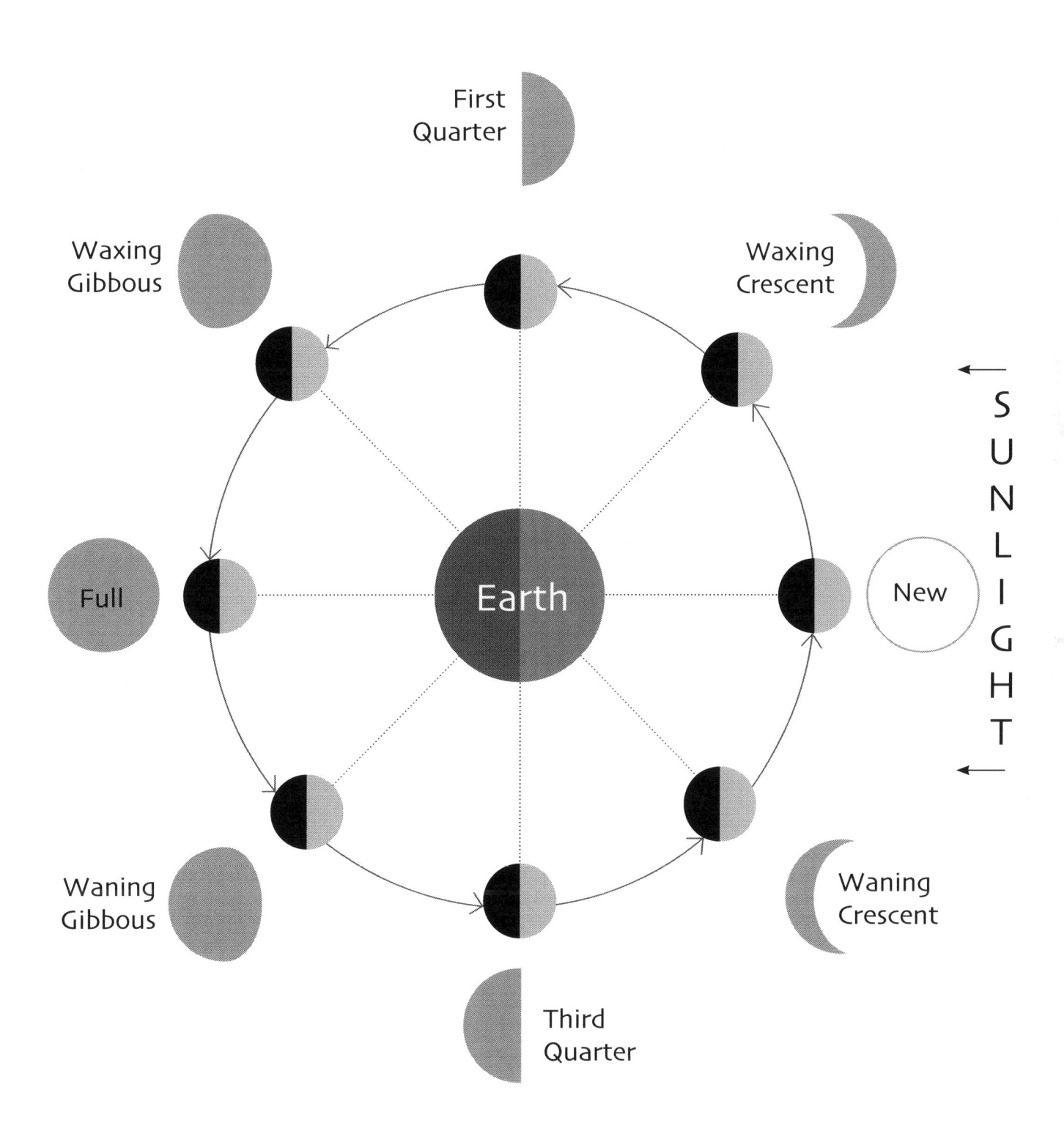

GENERIC SHEET 5

First Quarter

Waxing Crescent

Waxing Gibbous

Earth

New

Full

SUNLIGHT

Waning Gibbous

Waning Crescent

Third Quarter

CURRICULUM FOCUS • Famous journeys 65

Neil Armstrong questions and answers

When and where was Neil Armstrong born?

Neil Armstrong was born in August 5th, 1930 in a small town called Wapakoneta in the state of Ohio in the United States of America.

Why did the family move around so much when Neil was young?

Neil's father, Stephen Armstrong, worked for the state of Ohio as an auditor. It was his job to travel around towns and cities checking on finances to make sure they were being run correctly.

When did Neil Armstrong take his first flight?

In 1936 Neil and his father went to Warren Airport to see a special aeroplane there known as The Tin Goose. It was actually a three-engined Ford Trimotor made from aluminium. Following a conversation with the pilot they were offered a short flight.

In what other ways did Neil show an interest in aircraft and flying?

He read as much as he could about the subject in books and magazines and started to make detailed model aircraft in his spare time. He also began to study astronomy using a local observatory.

When did he learn to fly?

Flying lessons were expensive so, while at school, Neil had to take on a variety of different jobs to raise money. He cut the grass in a cemetery, worked in a pharmacy and washed planes at Port Koneta Airport. Lessons cost him nine dollars an hour. He took his first flying lesson at the age of 15 and got his student pilot's licence in 1946 on his 16th birthday.

What did Neil Armstrong decided to do when he left school?

He decided to study aeronautics, the science of flight, at university in Indiana, not very far away from home. His education was paid for through a US Navy scholarship. The aeronautical engineering course at the university was good and Neil enjoyed learning among people who shared exactly the same interests. He also joined the Naval Air Cadet programme.

What event caused him to change his plans?

During the second year of his four-year course at university a war started in Korea, a country near China in Asia. The Americans fought alongside the South Koreans. In 1950 Neil Armstrong was called up to fight. He became part of an all-jet fighter squadron that operated aboard the USS Essex in the Pacific Ocean.

What missions did he have to fly and what narrow escapes did he have?

Pilots had to fly low over enemy territory and damage bridges, factories and other targets. On one low-flying mission, Neil Armstrong flew into a metal cable that clipped off part of one of the aircraft's wings. On another mission he had to fly his damaged aircraft back to the USS Essex and land it safely on the deck of the aircraft carrier.

What happened after the war?

The war finally came to an end in 1953. Neil returned to Purdue University to complete his studies. He graduated from Purdue in January 1955 with a degree in aeronautical engineering. He first took a job at Lewis Flight Propulsion Laboratory and was then taken on as a test pilot at Edwards Air Force Base, California.

What work did Armstrong do at Edwards Air Force Base?

He flew prototypes of new aircraft and tested them to see how far they could go. Sometimes they checked to see how high the aircraft could fly. Other flights tested speed and turning ability. He also flew the X-15, a type of rocket plane that was launched from underneath a 'mother' aircraft. It would then fly to the edge of the atmosphere before gliding back to Earth.

What record did Neil Armstrong break?

In 1962 Armstrong's sixth flight in the X-15 took him to 63100 metres above the Earth's surface-the very edge of space. After the flight Neil Armstrong said, ' Space is the frontier, and that's where I intend to go.'

What was Armstrong's next move?

Later in 1962, the National Aeronautics and Space Administration (NASA) decided to change its priorities. It would no longer send rocket planes to the limits of the atmosphere but would aim instead to put a man on the Moon before the end of the decade. As a result, Neil Armstrong gave up his job as a test pilot and became a trainee astronaut.

What did Armstrong do on the Gemini Project?

The Gemini Project was part of the preparation work that had to be done before a spacecraft could be sent to the Moon. It was named Gemini after a constellation of stars that resemble a pair of twins. Armstrong acted as a back-up for Gemini 5 but then had his chance to go into space aboard Gemini 8.

What task did Gemini 8 have to perform?

Armstrong flew the mission on Gemini 8 in March 1966. With his co-pilot David Scott he had to dock with an unmanned satellite orbiting the Earth, the Agena. The astronauts had to carefully position the spacecraft in order to meet the satellite and then join the two together.

What difficulties did Armstrong have to overcome on Gemini 8?

After docking, the spacecraft and Agena began to spin out of control. Armstrong then separated the spacecraft but this made it turn even faster, often a full turn every second. Armstrong had to use the re-entry engines to steady the spacecraft. This meant aborting the rest of the mission and the two astronauts returned to Earth after only ten hours in space.

What did Neil Armstrong do next?

Neil became part of the Apollo missions, all aimed at putting a man on the Moon. He was part of the back-up crew for Apollo 8 and then, on January 9th, 1969, he was named in the Apollo 11 crew that would attempt a Moon landing.

Who were the other members of the Apollo 11 crew?

Armstrong would be the captain of Apollo 11 while the other members would be the experienced astronauts Edwin 'Buzz' Aldrin and Michael Collins.

What training did the Apollo 11 astronauts have to do?

The crew went through more training than anyone before. They used full-scale replicas of both the Command Module and the Lunar Module. NASA invented many problems for the crew to solve and during the spring and early summer of 1969 they spent over 400 hours working in simulators.

When and where did Apollo 11 blast off for the Moon?

On the morning of July 16th, 1969, Neil Armstrong was awake by 4.15 a.m. and after a breakfast of steak and eggs was helped into his spacesuit. Apollo 11 blasted off from Cape Kennedy, Florida at exactly 9.32 a.m. One million people had arrived in Florida to watch the take-off and an estimated twenty million watched on television.

How long did it take to get to the Moon?

The different stages of Apollo 11 took some four days to reach the Moon. At times the astronauts were travelling at about 40000 kilometres per hour.

Which astronauts landed on the Moon's surface?

Armstrong and Aldrin went aboard the Lunar Module called Eagle to travel down to the Moon's surface. Michael Collins remained in the mother ship, the Command Module Columbia, orbiting the Moon and ready to pick them up when they returned.

Who was first down the ladder of the Lunar Module?

The Lunar Module landed on the surface of the Moon a little after 3.15 p.m. on July 20th. Armstrong had to fly the spacecraft down onto the Moon by hand as the computer controls were not working well. By just after 9.30 p.m., Armstrong was walking down the ladder towards the surface of the Moon. Aldrin was to follow later.

What famous words did Armstrong say?

As Armstrong carefully put one boot on the lunar surface he said, 'That's one small step for (a) man, one giant leap for mankind.'

How long did Armstrong and Aldrin spend on the Moon?

The two astronauts spent about two hours on the Moon.

What did they do there?

They collected rock and dust samples for analysis back on Earth. They set up equipment for several experiments and tried out several different ways of moving around in the low-gravity environment.

What did they leave behind?

They planted an American flag on the Moon's surface. The flag had a special metal rod attached to it to open it out, as there is no wind on the Moon. An inscription on a plaque left at the Apollo 11 landing site read, 'Here men from the planet Earth first set foot on the Moon, July 1969. We came in peace for all mankind.'

When did the Command Module return to Earth?

The Command Module splashed down into the Pacific Ocean on July 24th about 1300 kilometres south west of Hawaii. They were lifted onto a helicopter and flown to the waiting aircraft carrier, the USS Hornet.

What special medal did Neil Armstrong receive?

All three astronauts received the Presidential Medal of Freedom, the highest civilian honour that an American citizen can be awarded. They were welcomed in huge parades in both New York and Chicago and a tour of twenty-eight world cities soon followed.

What did Neil Armstrong do in later life?

Neil continued to work for NASA for several years until, in 1971, he became Professor of Aerospace Engineering at Cincinnati University, Ohio. He also bought a diary farm nearby and left the university in 1979. Since then he has continued to live on his farm, work for a number of other companies and assist NASA when asked.

How did Neil Armstrong sum up the Apollo 11 mission to the Moon?

Neil Armstrong always remained puzzled about the great amount of personal publicity that he received after the Moonwalk. He was always anxious to stress that the event had been a team effort in which everyone involved should feel proud of their achievements.

Man on the Moon

LESSON PLAN 1

History objectives
- To find out about the life of the astronaut Neil Armstrong.
- To find out why he became so famous.

Resources

- Generic sheets 1, 2, 4, 6-8
- Activity sheets 1-3
- Witness for interview
- Large display poster of the Solar System
- Scissors, glue, sticky tape

Starting points: whole class

Start with a brainstorming session in which children tell each other as much as they know about the planets and space.

- What does the term Solar System mean?
- Which are the planets in the Solar System?
- In which order are the planets arranged?
- Which planets are close to each other?
- Which planets are similar in size?
- Which groups make up the inner planets and the outer planets?
- Why are they called this?

Mount large displays in the classroom that provide children as much information as possible about our neighbouring planets, their size, distance from the Earth, topological features and satellites etc.

Then focus on the Earth's only satellite, the Moon, and how it is visible on clear nights because it reflects light from the Sun. Find out what children know about putting a man on the Moon.

- When did man first walk on the Moon?
- Which country was able to do this first?
- What spacecraft was involved in the Moon flight?
- Who was the man who took the first steps on the Moon?
- How long did they stay on the Moon on this trip?
- What did they do while they were there?
- What did they bring back with them?
- What happened to these items?
- What did they leave behind?

It may be possible, at this stage, to introduce the class to an oral witness, a senior member of staff/grandparent, friend of the school who watched the first moon landing live on television in July 1969. They can tell children what happened and the amount of excitement it generated around the world.

Elicit that the astronaut Neil Armstrong, the commander of Apollo 11, was the man chosen to step onto the Moon's surface first. Use the Neil Armstrong timeline on Generic sheet 2 and the question and answer information on Generic sheets 5-7 to tell children more about the life of Neil Armstrong and how he came to be the first moonwalker.

Explain to children that in order to carry out his walk on the Moon, Neil Armstrong needed to wear a special suit. To survive in space you need a suit that protects the body from heat and cold and surrounds it with air to breathe. The suit has a backpack containing enough air, water and batteries to allow the astronaut to explore the Moon for several hours without being attached to the spacecraft for that length of time.

Show children pictures/photographs of Armstrong on the surface of the Moon and provide them with copies of Generic sheet 4.

Group activities

Activity sheet 1
On this sheet the children are provided with a full-length picture of Neil Armstrong. They also have a selection of important pieces of equipment that he needed to wear when he went on the first moonwalk. They have to cut out these items and dress the figure correctly. Once the figure is complete they should mount it on a separate piece of paper and label it using the words given at the bottom of the sheet. Talk with the children about the functions of each piece of equipment.

Activity sheet 2
This activity is the same as on Activity sheet 1 but children are also required to write short sentences at the bottom of the sheet explaining the important task that each item of equipment does. Again, the 'dressed' figure and the sentences could be cut out and mounted onto another piece of paper. It may help the children's writing if they discuss the functions of the items of equipment before putting pen to paper.

Activity sheet 3
More able children have the same clothing activity but the written element of the task is extended. Once the Neil Armstrong figure has been dressed they should write their own sentences about what each of the items of equipment does. In addition they should write any other information

about what Neil Armstrong and 'Buzz' Aldrin did during their two hours on the surface of the Moon in July 1969.

Plenary session

Ask an adult helper to go on the 'hot seat' and play the part of Neil Armstrong. Challenge children to ask the 'witness' questions as a way of revising what they know about Neil Armstrong and how he became famous. Questions might include some of the following.

- When were you born?
- Where were you born?
- When did you first become interested in flight?
- When did you learn to fly?
- Where did you study?
- What did you do in the Korean War?
- What jobs did you do later?
- Why did you want to become an astronaut?
- What was the most important part of the Apollo 11 mission?
- How did it feel to set foot on the Moon?
- How did it feel to get back home safely after the mission?
- How did it feel to be famous and recognised by everyone?

Ideas for support

The activity sheets require cutting, sticking and mounting on other sheets of paper and some children may benefit from help in this area and more time to complete the tasks. The function of many of the items of equipment on the activity sheets is fairly evident but the suit itself and the backpack may need more detailed explanation. The suit, for example, must be lightweight but strong. It must be airtight and protect the astronaut from both cold and heat. The backpack contains much other vital equipment including batteries, oxygen tanks, in-suit drinks containers, temperature control valve etc.

Ideas for extension

Neil Armstrong was a 'famous first' in the history of space travel–the first person to step on the surface of the Moon. Find out as much as possible about other 'famous firsts' in space.

- When was the first unmanned spacecraft launched?
- What was the first animal in space?
- Who was the first man in space?
- Who was the first woman in space?
- Who did the first walk in space?
- Who drove the first Moon buggy?
- When did the space shuttle first fly?
- Who launched the first space station?

Man on the moon

Name ....

ACTIVITY SHEET 1

Cut out the important parts of Neil Armstrong's special clothing for the moonwalk and stick them on his picture.

Label the picture using the words at the bottom of the sheet.

Word bank
space suit   backpack   gloves   boots   helmet   camera

CURRICULUM FOCUS • Famous journeys   71

ACTIVITY SHEET 2

Man on the moon

Name _____

Cut out the important parts of Neil Armstrong's special clothing for the moonwalk and stick them on his picture.

At the bottom of the sheet write a short sentence about what each item of equipment does.

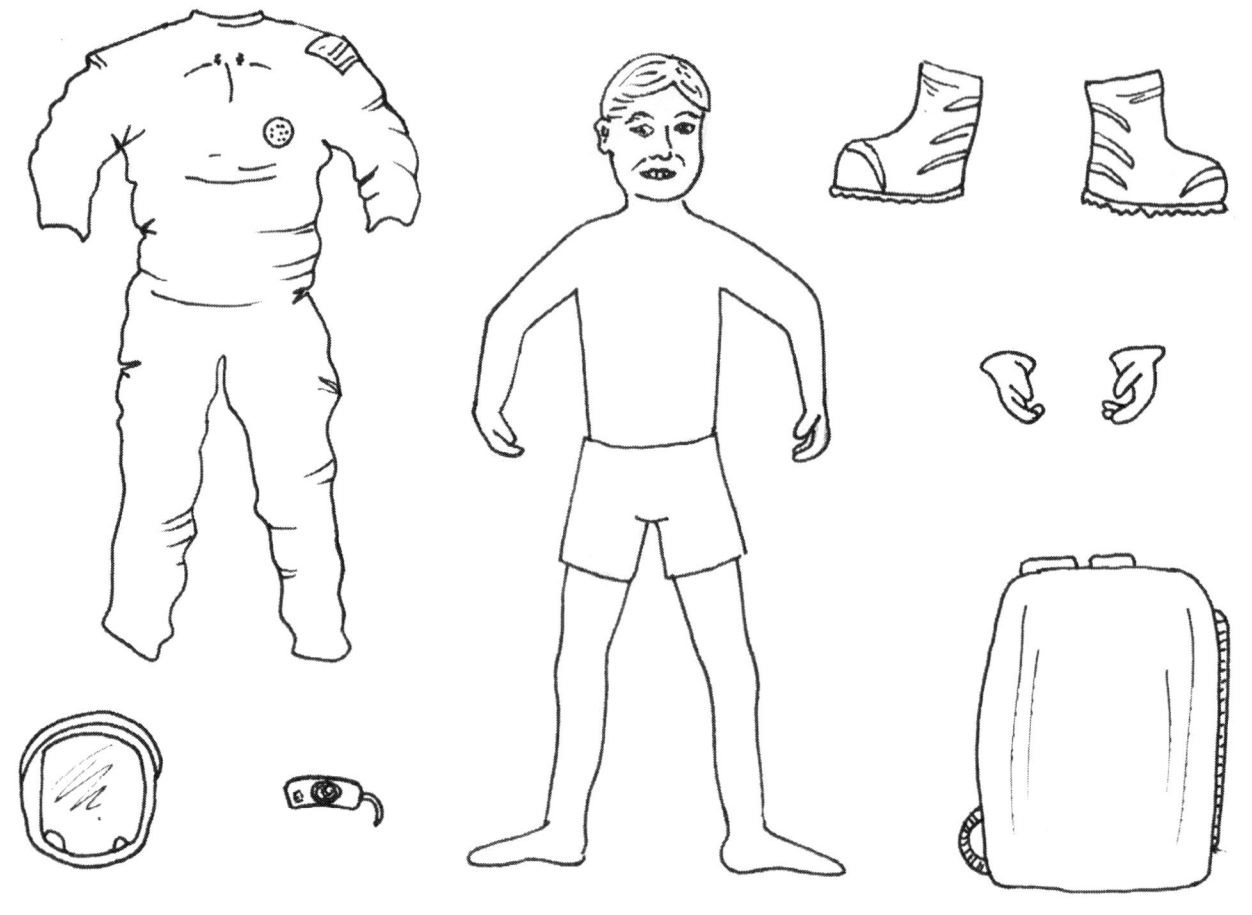

Gloves: _____

Boots: _____

Space suit: _____

Helmet: _____

Backpack: _____

Camera: _____

72 CURRICULUM FOCUS • Famous journeys

Man on the moon

3 ACTIVITY SHEET

Name ....

Cut out the important parts of Neil Armstrong's special clothing for the moonwalk and stick them on his picture.

On the bottom and the back of the sheet, write about what each item of equipment does.

Also write as much as you can find out about Armstrong's moonwalk and what he and 'Buzz' Aldrin did while they were on the surface of the Moon.

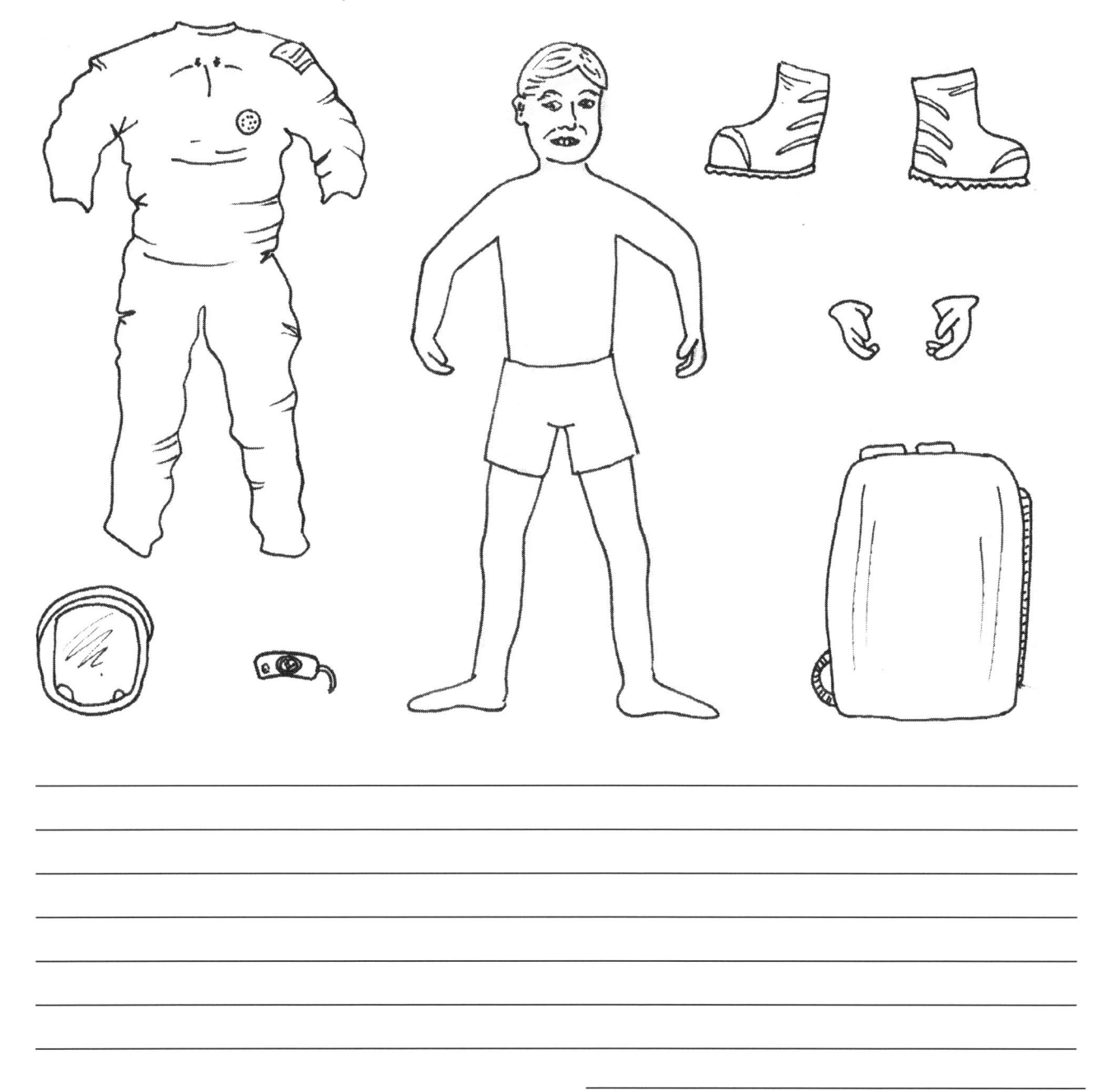

_____
_____
_____
_____
_____
_____

CURRICULUM FOCUS • Famous journeys **73**

LESSON PLAN 2

Captain's log

History objectives
- To find out more about the Apollo 11 mission to the Moon.
- To put into the correct sequence the key events of the history-making first walk on the surface of the Moon.

Resources

- Generic sheet 3
- Activity sheets 1-3

Starting points: whole class

Introduce the children to Generic sheet 3 and talk about what it shows. Emphasise that the Saturn 5 rocket ship that took Neil Armstrong and the other two astronauts to the Moon was made up of many stages.

There were in fact eight main sections. Seven of those sections were jettisoned somewhere in space and only one of them returned safely with the astronauts to Earth.

Say that the first three stages were mainly fuel tanks and rocket motors needed to drive the spaceship away from the Earth's gravity into space and to start its journey to the Moon.

Then consider the functions of the parts of the spaceship where members of the crew would live and work during the journey, the Service Module, the Command Module and the Lunar Module (two parts).

The job of the Service Module was to complete the journey to the Moon, orbit it and then take the astronauts most of the way home. The Command Module was for the last part of the journey and would splash down into the Pacific Ocean at the end of the journey. The Lunar Module was in two parts. Both would go down onto the surface of the Moon but only one would lift back off. The other part would be left behind. The other half of the Lunar Module would be ditched on the return home.

In simple terms, run through the sequence of events in the Apollo 11 mission. Talk about each step slowly and stress the importance of each stage having to follow another if the mission was to be successful.

- July 16th: Astronauts dress early in space suits; Saturn 5 blasts off for the Moon; stages 1 and 2 drop away; spaceship sets course for the Moon at a speed of 3800 km/hour.
- July 19th: Stage 3 separates; start orbit of the Moon.
- July 20th: Descent to the Moon; Armstrong sets foot on the Moon; astronauts work for two hours on the Moon's surface; both parts of the Lunar Module ditched.
- July 21st: Start return journey to Earth; Service Module cast adrift.
- July 24th: Command Module splashed down in the Pacific Ocean; astronauts picked up and taken to the USS Hornet.

Tell children that explorers who have been on history making journeys have usually kept a log or record book of the events. (Refer them to Amelia Earhart, Amundsen and Scott on their journey to the South Pole and Ellen MacArthur sailing around the world.)

They are to imagine they are the Apollo 11 commander Neil Armstrong and they are going to write logbook entries for some of the things that happened during the Apollo 11 mission. Their eyewitness accounts should not only focus on what happened but also what they could see and hear. They should also include the feelings they experienced at certain stages during the journey especially first contact with the Moon's surface and safe splashdown in the Pacific Ocean.

Group activities

Activity sheet 1
This sheet is aimed specifically at children who may need some help with their writing. Two key events have been chosen, Neil Armstrong setting foot on the Moon and the return of the astronauts to Earth. Encourage children to use short sentences containing as much detailed description as they can. A word bank is provided on the bottom of the sheet to help them with spelling. Provide other words that may be helpful.

Activity sheet 2
This sheet requires three extracts from Neil Armstrong's log. In addition to the two events on the previous activity sheet, the Saturn 5 blast off for the Moon is also included. Emphasise the importance of including how they would feel if they were in Armstrong's place as well as describing what is happening and what he could see and hear. Some help may be needed with spelling, especially if examples of specialised vocabulary are included, for example, orbit, lunar, satellite, module etc.

Activity sheet 3
This sheet is intended for more able children and gives them greater independence when they are writing their log entries about the Apollo 11 mission. They are given blank

logbook pages and should provide their own dated events. Encourage them to choose the more exciting happenings in the mission. It may be necessary to discuss a number of the events with them first e.g. blast off, orbiting the Moon, touching down on the Moon's surface, heading for home, splashing down in the Pacific etc. Encourage good use of vocabulary throughout, especially the use of appropriate verbs and colourful descriptions.

Plenary session

Select examples of the work of each of the three activity groups and make a classroom display of the finished work. Discuss the way in which children have written the first-hand logbook accounts. Have they captured how the astronauts must have felt at the time?

Revise key issues raised during the session. Massive rockets blast the multi-section spacecraft off to the Moon but only a small capsule comes back to Earth. Is it justified to leave the debris of all the discarded stages in space? Recap on the sequence of events that happened during the mission. It was vital that one stage followed on successfully from another. What potential difficulties could there have been? What do children consider to be the most dangerous part of the mission? Was the spending of millions of dollars to put a man on the Moon really justified? What do children consider to have been the major benefits?

Ideas for support

Provide plenty of visual stimulation to help with the first-hand eyewitness accounts of the Apollo 11 mission. Provide individual or class word banks to help with vocabulary. Among the key words that will benefit from discussion are some of the following: lunar, module, jettison, booster, rocket, stage, re-entry, descent, commander, space, orbit, gravity, astronaut, fuel, crater, splashdown.

Emphasise the importance of good punctuation in the accounts and also neat handwriting and presentation to make the diary accounts appealing.

Ideas for extension

Research the other manned lunar landings that happened after Neil Armstrong's history making journey. Apollo's 11, 12, 14, 16 and 17 all put men on the Moon, the last successful landing being made in 1972. (There were problems with the Apollo 13 mission and the proposed landing on the Moon was aborted.) What astronauts were involved on the Apollo missions? What jobs did they carry out on the Moon? What did they achieve? What information do we know about the Moon now that we did not know before? Manned missions to the Moon are planned but, as yet, they are not underway. The Moon continues to be free to all nations to explore for peaceful purposes.

Captain's log

Name ....

Imagine Neil Armstrong kept a log of the Apollo 11 mission.

What did he do, see, hear and feel during the journey?

Fill in the log pages for these two events. Use the word bank at the bottom of the page to help you.

July 20th, 1969: I set foot on the surface of the Moon.

_____
_____
_____
_____
_____
_____

July 24th, 1969: Command Module splashes down in the Pacific Ocean.

_____
_____
_____
_____
_____
_____

Word bank

space suit   backpack   boots   ladder   camera   helmet   dust   rock   flag   crater   radio
lunar module   parachute   raft   rocket   motor   rescue   ship   astronaut

CURRICULUM FOCUS • Famous journeys

Captain's log

ACTIVITY SHEET 2

Name ....

Imagine Neil Armstrong kept a log of the Apollo 11 mission.

What did he do, see, hear and feel during the mission?

Fill in the log entries for these three important events.

July 16th, 1969: Saturn 5 blasts off for the Moon.
_____
_____
_____
_____

July 20th, 1969: I set foot on the surface of the Moon.
_____
_____
_____
_____

July 24th, 1969: Command Module splashes down in the Pacific Ocean.
_____
_____
_____
_____

CURRICULUM FOCUS • Famous journeys

Captain's log

Name ....

Imagine Neil Armstrong kept a log of the Apollo 11 mission.

What did he do, see, hear and feel during the mission?

Choose three key events from the mission and make up log entries on the blank pages given describing in detail what happened.

Lunar study

LESSON PLAN 3

History objectives
- To find out more about the Moon as a satellite of the Earth.
- To find out how centuries of study have enabled scientists and astronomers to find out more about the Moon.

Resources

- Large pictures of the Moon
- Diagram of the main phases of the Moon. Generic sheet 5
- Picture of Galileo
- Diagrams of early telescopes
- Picture of large modern radio-telescope
- Activity sheet 1-3

Starting points: whole class

Start by telling children that the word 'Moon' is related to the Latin and Greek words for month. Make connections here with the way in which the phases of the Moon have always been used for measuring time. The Latin word for 'Moon' is Luna, from which we get the word lunar–meaning anything connected to the Moon.

Then discuss the following factfile of information with the children to see how much they know about the Moon already.

- The Moon orbits the Earth in about twenty-seven days.
- The Moon's orbit of the Earth is slightly squashed. It is in the shape of an ellipse.
- The Moon is reckoned to be 4.5 billion years old.
- The Moon is about 384 500km from the Earth.
- The Moon's diameter is 3476km.
- It would take 13 hours to get to the Moon by fast rocket ship.
- The surface area of the Moon is about the same as that of Africa.
- The Moon's surface is covered with craters, valleys, mountains and plains.
- Meteors colliding with the surface of the Moon have caused these large craters.
- Footprints left by astronauts on the surface of the Moon could last for 10 million years.
- There is no wind or weather on the Moon so nothing erodes.
- Evidence of water has been found on the Moon during the last two years.

Tell children that astronomers and scientists have been studying the Moon since the earliest times. The Babylonians, the Ancient Greeks and the Chinese got close to accurately calculating its size and its distance from the Earth. They also realised that the Moon did not produce its own light but that it reflected light from the Sun.

Also tell them that one of the first scientists to view the Moon through a telescope was the famous Italian Galileo Galilei (1564–1642). Show children a picture of Galileo and what the telescopes of that period would have looked like. Note the similarities and differences between these early telescopes and the large radio-telescopes that are used today. Galileo included drawings of the Moon in his book Siderus Nuncius. He noted that the Moon was not smooth but had mountains and large craters as well as plains and valleys. He called some of the hollows and depressions seas–the name still used today–because he thought that they might be filled with water.

Other astronomers like Thomas Harriott (1560–1621), Giovanni Riccioli (1598–1671) and Francesco Maria Grimaldi (1618–1663) also drew lunar maps. They gave the large craters many of the names we still use today. They also began to use the name selenography, the official title for the study of the Moon. The name comes from Selene, the Greek goddess of the Moon.

Update children by telling that over the last thirty years, accurate and sophisticated camera equipment has been used to get closer to the surface of the Moon so that it can be photographed in greater detail. The always-invisible far side of the Moon has been photographed, many rocks and dust samples have been collected and scientific equipment has been left on the Moon's surface so that it can relay information back to the Earth.

Activity sheet 1
On this activity sheet children are shown pictures of five of the main phases of the Moon. They label each of the five pictures correctly and then place the phases in the correct sequence. The names of the different phases are listed at the bottom of the sheet for the children to copy.

Activity sheet 2
On this activity sheet, all the eight main phases of the Moon are shown in diagram form. Again children are asked to label each phase carefully and then place the phases in the correct order starting with the new Moon.

Activity sheet 3
This activity sheet, for more able children, requires them to complete a moon observation sheet over a period of about a month. Empty boxes are provided on the sheet for

children to draw their small diagrams in. If they are unable to see the Moon on a particular night, children are asked to write 'too cloudy' but the details about the Moon's phases published each day in newspapers might be used to fill in any gaps that occur.

Plenary

Revise some of the important pieces of information given in the factfile to check children have remembered key facts about the Moon. How far away from the Earth is it? What is its size? How old is it? What is its surface like? Also ask them to explain why we know so much about the Moon since the Apollo 11 mission took place.

Put an unlabelled chart up on the wall or use diagrams on the whiteboard to test children's knowledge of the main phases of the Moon. Concentrate particularly on getting the phases in the right sequence.

Ask one of the children you worked on Activity sheet 3 to talk about how successfully they managed to record the phases of the Moon over a period of about a month. How many nights was the weather clear enough to get an accurate view?

Ideas for support

Guidance and help will need to be given when children are using reference sources to gather information about the Moon. Information may need to be simplified for some when making factfiles and word banks will be needed to help with spelling. Waxing and waning will need to be explained and the meaning of the word gibbous. (Waxing is when the visible illuminated part of the Moon increases in size. Waning is when this section gets smaller. Gibbous means when the illuminated part of the Moon is greater than a semicircle but smaller than a circle.) Since large numbers are often involved in discussions about space travel, help will be needed with approximating, rounding off and scaling down. Enlist the help of parents/carers as one of the tasks, the Moon phases' data collection table, will need to be done outside of school time.

Ideas for extension

Having established that children understand that the Earth has only one satellite (Moon), find out more about the satellites (Moons) of the other main planets in the Solar System. Mars has two, for example, Deimos and Phobus while Pluto has three, Charon, Nox and Hydra. Jupiter and Saturn have more than sixty each. Contrast these with Mercury and Venus that has no Moons at all.

In company with Galileo, find out more about the work of other important astronomers of the period like Nicolaus Copernicus (1473-1543), Johannes Kepler (1571-1630) and Tycho Brahe (1546-1601).

Lunar study

ACTIVITY SHEET 1

Name ....

Here are five of the main phases of the Moon.

Give each its correct name and then put them into the right sequence.

Word bank
full moon   waxing crescent   first quarter   waxing gibbous   waning crescent

CURRICULUM FOCUS • Famous journeys **81**

Lunar study

Name ....

Here are the eight main phases of the Moon.

Give them their correct names and then place them in the right sequence.

Word bank
first quarter   new moon   waning crescent   waxing gibbous   full moon   last quarter
waning gibbous   waxing crescent

82   CURRICULUM FOCUS • Famous journeys

Lunar study

Name ....

Moon observation sheet: Draw a small picture of how the Moon looks in the sky each night for the next month. Write 'too cloudy' if the Moon is not visible on any night.

ACTIVITY SHEET 3

CURRICULUM FOCUS • Famous journeys

Ellen MacArthur

TEACHERS' NOTES

Over the line

Shortly after 10 p.m. on February 7th, 2005, Ellen MacArthur on her yacht B&Q crossed an imaginary finishing line in the water off the coast of France. She had become the fastest person ever to sail around the world single-handed and the youngest woman ever to do so.

Her trimaran B&Q had sailed over 50600 kilometres at an average speed of almost sixteen knots. The circumnavigation had taken a little over seventy-one days and had beaten the existing record by more than a day. During the voyage Ellen had been on the lookout constantly during every day and night and she had had no more than twenty minutes sleep at any one time. She had survived mountainous seas, gale-force winds and drifting icebergs.

Later when Ellen reached Falmouth in Cornwall the scenes were euphoric. The new record and the ones she had broken previously made this diminutive twenty-eight year old individual Britain's top female sailor and one of the high ever achievers in British sailing.

She wrote on reaching the end of such a tremendous voyage, 'When I crossed the line, I felt like collapsing on the cockpit floor and just falling asleep. The pure fact that you can actually let go, that when you cross the line it's over, it's just over, and you don't have to worry any more, that was the biggest emotion-huge relief.'

Ellen's willingness to continually push further and harder has served as an inspiration and role model for young sailors and yachtsmen everywhere. She has done more than any other to dispel the myth that sailing is mainly a pursuit for the wealthy middle class and she has conveyed to millions of 'landlubbers' the appeal and enthusiasm of travelling at sea in small boats.

Early life

Ellen MacArthur, born July 8th, 1976, was brought up in the village of Whatstandwell near Matlock in Derbyshire, almost as far away from the sea as it is possible to get in 'middle' England. She lived there with her parents, both schoolteachers, and two brothers, Fergus and Lewis. The family lived on a smallholding. There was plenty of room for adventure type games and family pets to take care of. Later it seemed likely that a career looking after animals might be possible.

A desire to follow in the footsteps of her idol at the time, Sophie Burke, and a passion for reading the children's boating story Swallows and Amazons by Arthur Ransome is said to have first stimulated her interest in sailing. She was further inspired as a youngster when an aunt, Aunt Thea, introduced her to sailing on the east coast of England aboard a boat called Cabaret. Following these short trips to sea, Ellen was determined to own her own boat.

She saved money at every opportunity and several years later, with the help of a monetary gift from her grandmother, she was able to buy her own boat. It was a three-metre long dinghy that she re-named Threepenny Bit after the small pre-decimal coin. To celebrate her tenth birthday her parents paid for her to go on a sailing course at Rutland Water. She was one of the youngest there and although she capsized on numerous occasions the experience taught her the basic skills of handling a sailing boat on water. Several years later Ellen acquired another boat, Kestrel, on which she worked hard during two summers in order to get it into tip-top condition. So single-minded and determined was Ellen's approach that her parents decided that she should learn to sail properly and enrolled her for a course at the David King Nautical School in Hull.

Further inspiration came during a period when, before taking some important school exams, she was confined to bed with an attack of glandular fever. Ellen spent much of her time watching the Whitbread Round the World Yacht Race on television and from then on her career path in sailing was decided.

By the time she was seventeen years old, Ellen had graduated to a new and larger vessel, a six-metre sailing boat named Iduna. According to Ellen it was 'love at first sight' when she saw the boat and in 1995 at the age of eighteen she sailed Iduna around the coast of Great Britain solo. The journey took Ellen about four and half months to complete, as there were several lengthy stopovers on the way. By this time she had already decided to devote herself full-time to sailing. Following intensive training, she achieved her Royal Yachting Association Yachtmaster qualification and become a RYA instructor at the David King School.

Competition sailing

Ellen was determined to try her hand at competition sailing especially after she had been voted British Young Sailor of the Year in 1995. Trying to find financial backing for her exploits through sponsorship proved difficult however especially, when, on one occasion, over two thousand letters to potential sponsors resulted in only two replies.

With support in Britain lacking, Ellen turned instead to France where, in 1997 as an unknown twenty year-old, she

CURRICULUM FOCUS • Famous journeys

crossed the Channel to buy a seven-metre yacht called Le Poisson. The boat was re-fitted in a French boatyard where Ellen often camped out next to it in order to see the work done. The need to communicate with local workers also forced her into becoming a fluent French speaker. Once complete, Le Poisson was entered for the Mini Transat solo race across the Atlantic from Martinique in the West Indies to Brest in France. Ellen finished her first solo race in just thirty-three days, took seventeenth place and won the admiration of the French people.

Further competitions followed. In 1998 Ellen managed to secure sponsorship from the retail group Kingfisher who funded her move to an Open 50 yacht that completed the gruelling Route du Rhum race across the Atlantic Ocean. She won her class and finished fifth in the event overall-an achievement that won her the title Yachtsman of the Year.

Early in 2000, her new boat, named Kingfisher after the sponsoring company, was launched in New Zealand. After early trials it was sailed back to Europe so that Ellen could get used to handling the vessel on the open sea. The sponsors continued to be impressed and with more backing Ellen sailed competitively from Plymouth, England to Rhodes, USA in fourteen days, twenty-three hours and eleven minutes. This still remains the current record for a single-handed mono-hull east to west passage of the Atlantic and also the record for a single-handed crossing by a woman in any vessel.

Kingfisher was soon in action again as Ellen decided to enter the Vendee Globe, a single-handed race around the world that started late in 2000 and finished early in the following year. During the course of the race, Ellen had to carry out a number of urgent repairs including having to climb the mast to tend to the yacht's mainsail. Other damage slowed her down but she still became the youngest woman sailor to complete a circumnavigation, finishing the race in a time of ninety-four days, eight hours and twenty-two minutes. Placed first among the mono-hull boats and second overall, she was also given national recognition when awarded the MBE (Member of the British Empire) for services to the sport of sailing. She also won the Helen Rollason Award for courage and achievement in the face of adversity and was runner-up in the BBC Sports Personality of the Year Award, a notable accolade for someone representing a non-mainstream sport.

In November 2002 it was back to the Route du Rhum race between St. Malo in France and the island of Guadeloupe in the Caribbean. This time no one was to stand in her way and, despite almost losing the mast and damaging the rudder, she came in first at the helm of Kingfisher in a new record time for the mono-hull class.

It was during 2003 that Ellen decided to switch to multi-hull boats, catamarans (two hulls) and trimarans (three hulls). She sailed first with the Frenchman Alain Gautier and then, later in the year, on a fully crewed vessel, made an attempt on the Jules Verne round-the-world record. This time however luck was against her and the bid had to be abandoned when the giant catamaran, Kingfisher 2, was dis-masted in the middle of the Indian Ocean.

It was in the same year that Ellen founded The Ellen MacArthur Trust, an organisation that provides sailing trips for children with leukaemia and similar illnesses. Based at Cowes in the Isle of Wight, the children sail on large cruising yachts. They live on board as the vessels travel to a different port each night. It allows them to take part in an exciting outdoor adventure break and, for a short time, to think about other things than their illness. Ellen joins the sailing trips whenever possible and other well-known sailors also help.

The big prize

Ellen took on her biggest challenge in November 2004. She set out on an attempt to beat the round-the-world solo record that had been set earlier in the year by the Frenchman Francis Joyon. He had been the first sailor ever to circumnavigate the world in a multi-hull and Ellen MacArthur wanted to be the next one to achieve it. This time Ellen was sailing in the trimaran B&Q, another boat named after the event's main sponsor. The yacht, built mainly in Australia, weighed over eight tonnes. It was almost twenty-three metres in length and just over sixteen metres wide. The mast stretched over thirty metres into the sky. The construction of the yacht had been truly an international affair with a total of six different countries involved in its building. In addition to Australia (main hull, floats, beams and fittings) there were contributions from New Zealand (mast and rigging), United Kingdom (rudder and foils), United States of America and France (sails) and Italy (deck hardware). The main advantage of using a multi-hull was that they have the ability to travel faster on the high seas. On the downside, they are prone to capsizing.

B&Q crossed the start line soon after eight o'clock on the morning of November 28th, 2004. The race was on but it would be tough. Only two weeks into the voyage the generator broke down. Ellen was forced to survive on freeze-dried meals and desalinated seawater. Perhaps, worst of all, was the fact that the sea was so unpredictable that it needed watching all the time. Ellen slept in small bursts only, usually lasting no more than about twenty minutes. Icebergs floated close to B&Q on several occasions. The winds could reach gale force in some locations while a period of five days with hardly any wind at all slowed her down considerably. A major problem occurred when a sail broke away from the top of the mast. Ellen was forced to climb to the top to fix it and got very bruised and battered in the process.

MacArthur's fans followed her progress on the official website. At times she lost her lead over Joyon's record because of wind conditions but then a storm would push her ahead and she would make excellent progress again. Early in 2005 she wrote of the storms she faced in the South Atlantic. 'Everything is creaking and groaning and smashing and grinding, it's just terrible. You go over three waves and you close your eyes and hope it's okay. Then the fourth one, whack. I'm sure something is going to break.' One of the most frightening incidents during the voyage involved a near collision with a big whale. 'I saw a whale very, very close to the boat. It was just in front of us and we sailed right over it. It went underneath our starboard float and, as it went underneath us, it blew its air tanks and its nose came out of the water.'

The day after crossing the finishing line, Ellen sailed into the harbour at Falmouth in Cornwall to be met by some eight thousand well-wishers. Joyon's record had been beaten by a whole day and further congratulations were to follow. A message came from the Prime Minister, Tony Blair, and the Queen made Ellen a Dame Commander of the British Empire. It is believed that, at the age of twenty-eight, she is the youngest person ever to receive the honour. Despite her individual achievement in breaking the record, Ellen MacArthur was always lavish in her praise of those who had helped her. 'I work with an unbelievable team and am supported by some incredible people. I'm not just out there doing it for me, I'm doing it for everybody.'

Note: Ellen's record was broken in January 2008 when Francis Joyon again sailed around the world solo, clipping more than fourteen days off the time. Ellen travelled to France to be one of the first people there to congratulate him, stressing, as always, records are made to be broken.

The future

Ellen MacArthur has written widely about her experiences in a number of books including Taking on the World (autobiography), Full Circle and Race Against Time (dealing specifically with the round-the-world record breaking voyage).

She continues to lives in Cowes on the Isle of Wight which is also home to Offshore Challenges, the company she is still most closely associated with. She also continues to work with the Ellen MacArthur Trust, the charity that she set up to provide sailing breaks for young people recovering from cancer and other serious illnesses.

In 2009 Ellen announced that she would no longer be focusing on competitive sailing and, following a visit to Antarctica and the Southern Ocean, said she intends to devote her time to environmental issues especially non-sustainable energy resources. Through a charitable foundation, she hopes to promote a better understanding of the facts and help people to draw their own conclusions about the global challenges we all face. The aim of the foundation will be to concentrate on three main areas: Communicating the facts and making them relevant to people. Working as an agent for change within business. Setting up projects with specific measurable objectives.

Ellen MacArthur

Timeline of the main events and achievements in the life of Ellen MacArthur

1970	• Born **July 8, 1976**, in Derbyshire, England
1980	• First sailing trip on Cabaret in **1981**
	• Buys her first boat in **1985**
1990	• Completed solo sail around the British Isles in **1995**
	• Finished in seventeenth place in a transatlantic race in **1997**
	• Won first place in her class in the France-to-Guadeloupe Route du Rhum challenge, **1998**
	• Wins Yachtsman of the Year Award in **1999**
2000	• Placed second in the Vendée Globe race in **2001**
	• Set new world record in the Route du Rhum race in **2002**
	• Set new world record for fastest circumnavigation of the globe as solo sailor in **2005**
	• Member of the Order of the British Empire in **2002**
	• Created dame by Queen Elizabeth II in **2005**

Route followed by Ellen MacArthur

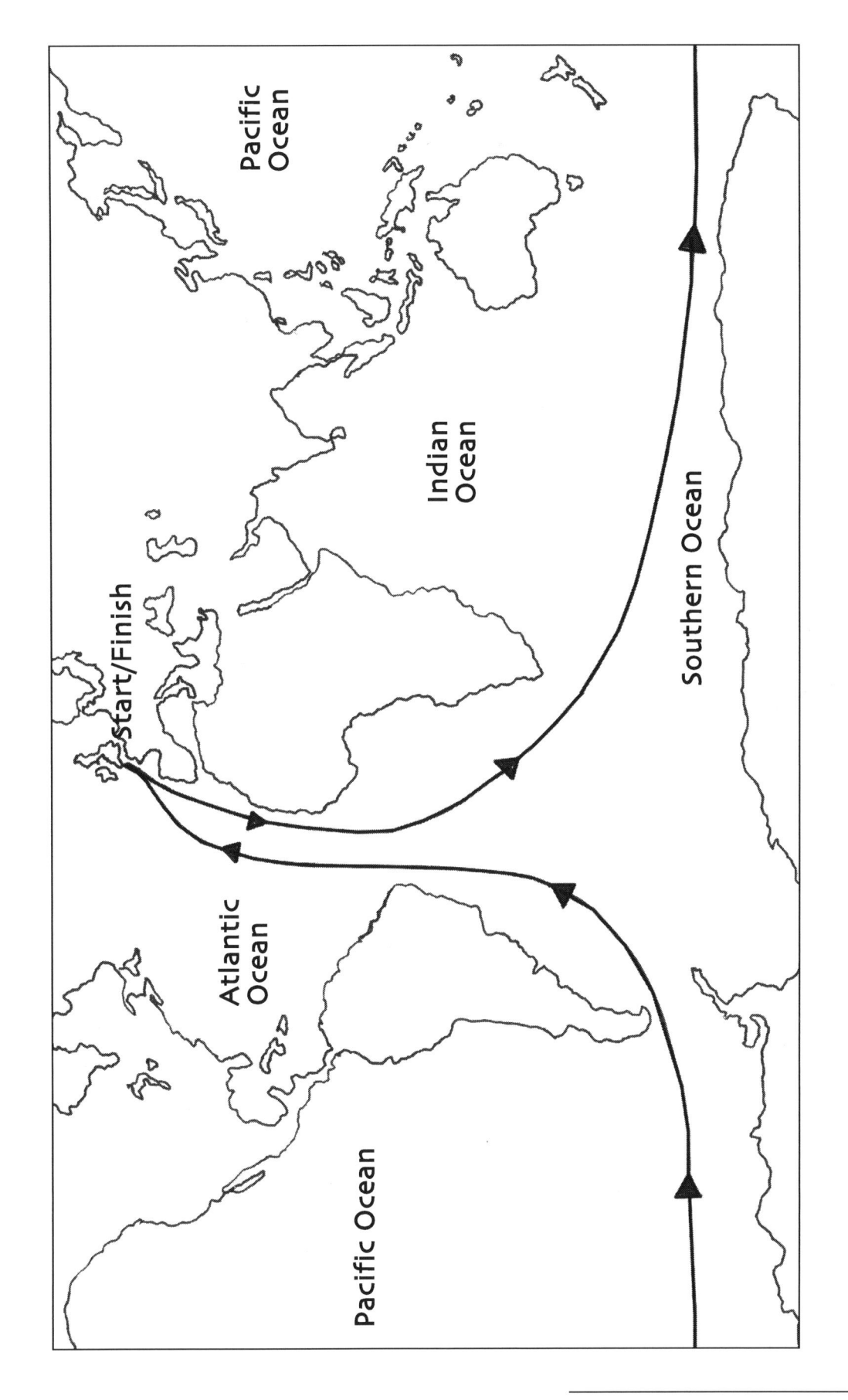

Ellen MacArthur quotes

Courage is not having the energy to go on, it is going on when you do not have the energy.

When I was out there, I was never alone.
There was always a team of people behind me, in mind if not in body.

You don't fear for your life in the middle of a storm. You can't really afford to.

On having the record taken away from her... Francis has set us another high benchmark.
The chances of breaking it are very slim but if we don't try we won't know.

A record is nothing if not shared. I'm proud of the record but
I'm even more proud to be working with the best team in the world.

When it's a race, you just can't stop. I would be easy to say 'chill out' when you're
tired but you never have to lose the goal of the finish line.
That's what you set out do and that's what you stick to.

The Southern Ocean is unique. It wants everything.
When you have nothing left, it wants twice as much again.

Fear almost certainly kept me alive in the Southern Ocean. It keeps you focused and vigilant.

All that round-the-world sailing has taught me is that I must be crazy.

On spotting icebergs... Never in my life have I experienced
such beauty and fear at the same time.

On being at sea for long spells... One of the things I miss most is the countryside.
I haven't seen a tree for nearly three months.

People often ask if I miss the sea. Sure I do but when I'm at sea I always miss the fields and
farms, so I think I take Derbyshire a little bit less for granted than I might otherwise do.

On her yacht B&Q... When you spend so much time pushing, caring for,
cajoling and maintaining a beautiful racing machine like this you get very close.
She's looked after me and I look after her, I haven't been lonely at all.

I'm not brave. I just choose to do things that push me very hard. That's not bravery, that's
choice. Now real bravery is in the kids I go sailing with, kids with cancer and leukaemia. When
you see what they deal with every day with big smiles and such energy, it's such a lesson.

Sailing taught me how to manage resources. Now I want to spread the word.

5
GENERIC SHEET

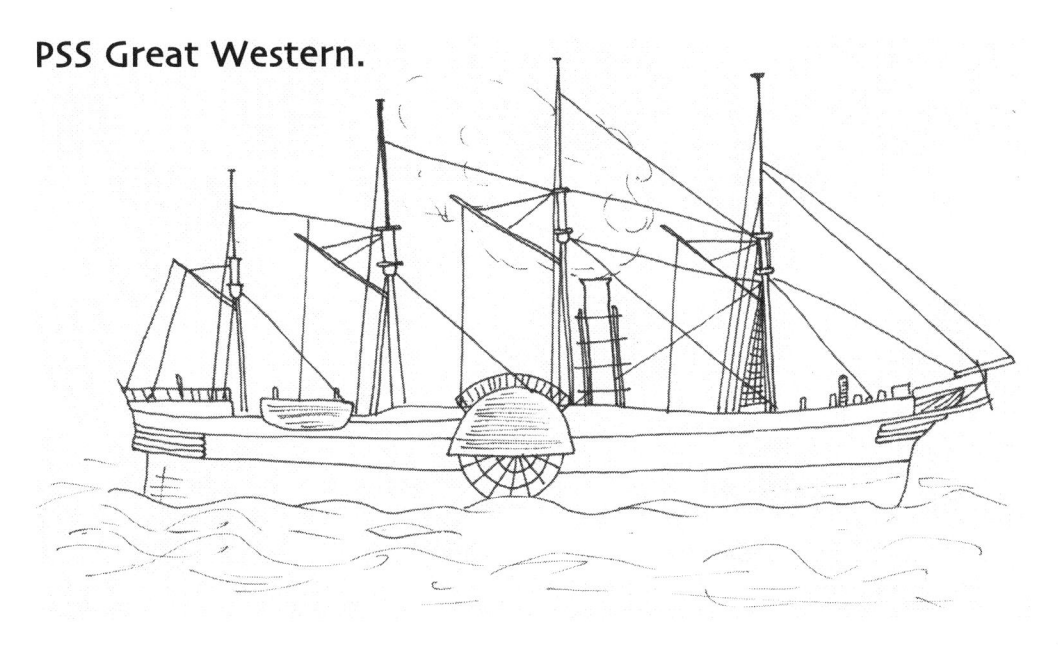

PSS Great Western.

Viking longship

Drake's The Golden Hind

CURRICULUM FOCUS • Famous journeys

Ellen MacArthur questions and answers

When was Ellen MacArthur born?

She was born on July 8th, 1976.

Where did she live as a child?

She lived in the village of Whatstandwell near Matlock in Derbyshire. She lived with her parents, both teachers, and her two brothers, Fergus and Lewis.

What children's book first interested her in boats and sailing?

She read a well-known children's book called Swallows and Amazons by the author Arthur Ransome.

Who first took Ellen sailing?

She made her first sailing trips when the family went on holiday to visit her Aunt Thea.

What was the boat called and where did they sail?

Aunt Thea's boat was called Cabaret and they did their sailing off the east coast of England.

What was Ellen's first boat called?

Ellen saved all her spare money to buy her first boat and her grandmother also helped with a gift. She named the boat Threepenny Bit after the small pre-decimal coin worth 3d.

Where did Ellen learn to sail properly?

Because her parents could see she was so interested they paid for her to attend a sailing course at Rutland Water. She was the youngest one on the course. During the time she was there, she capsized many times but she quickly learnt the basic skills of handling a small sailing boat. Later she went to the David King Nautical School in Hull.

How did Ellen learn more about round-the-world sailing?

Just before she was due to take some exams at school, she caught glandular fever. It meant she had to stay at home. To pass the time she watched coverage of the Whitbread Round the World Yacht Race on television and followed the progress of the competitors.

What boat did she buy when she was seventeen?

It was a six-metre sailing yacht called Iduna. Apparently, when she first saw the boat it was 'love at first sight'.

What trip did Ellen MacArthur make in 1995 at the age of eighteen?

She sailed Induna around the coast of Great Britain solo. The journey took Ellen four and half months, as there were several long stopovers during the voyage. Storms and huge waves kept her in port at Hartlepool for some time and when she reached Montrose in Scotland she was ill for several days.

What award did Ellen MacArthur win that year?

There were journalists and photographers waiting to meet her when Ellen arrived in Hull at the end of the voyage. As a result, she became famous throughout the country and was finally awarded the title British Young Sailor of the Year.

What boat did Ellen buy in France?

Finding support difficult to find in Britain, Ellen crossed the Channel to France where she bought a boat called Le Poisson. She had to do much of the re-building of the boat herself and often worked long hours in the boatyard. So she could communicate with the workers in France, Ellen had to learn French very quickly.

When Le Poisson was re-built, what race did Ellen enter?

Ellen competed in the Mini Transat. Boats raced across the Atlantic between France and the island of Martinique in the Caribbean. It is a very dangerous race that has claimed a number of lives in the past. Ellen finished the race in thirty-three days and took seventeenth place. More important, the event attracted the attention of sponsors who would be able to help her in future races.

What result did Ellen get in the Route du Rhum?

In 1998, now sponsored by the giant retail group, Kingfisher, Ellen entered the Route du Rhum race, again across the Atlantic. This time she won her class, finished fifth overall and won the title of Yachtsman of the Year.

What was the Vendee Globe?

The Vendee Globe was a solo round-the-world sailing race that Ellen took part in during 2000-2001. Despite several setbacks, Ellen still became the youngest woman sailor to complete a circumnavigation. She completed the race in about ninety-four days. Ellen was placed first among the mono-hull boats and second overall. As a result of her achievement she was made an MBE (Member of the British Empire).

What new boat did Ellen change to now?

It was during 2003 that Ellen decided to change to a catamaran boat named Kingfisher 2. Along with a crew of fourteen, Ellen attempted to beat the round-the-world record in the Jules Verne event. This time luck was against her and they were forced to abandon the race when the mast broke in the Indian Ocean.

What is the Ellen MacArthur Trust?

During the summer of 2000 Ellen had worked for a French charity called A Chacun son Cap (Everyone has a Goal). The charity took children who had leukaemia, or were recovering from it, out sailing. Ellen was so moved by the children that she decided to set-up a similar charity in Britain called The Ellen MacArthur Trust. The Trust operates from Cowes on the Isle of Wight. It allows the children to experience an adventure break and helps them think about something other than their illness for a short time.

Who previously held the round-the-world solo sailing record in 2004?

The record was held by the French sailor Francis Joyon who made the trip earlier in 2004. He had been the first to go round the world in a multi-hull boat.

In which boat did Ellen set out to try and break Francis Joyon's record?

This time Ellen was sailing in a new trimaran (three hulls) called B&Q. It weighed over eight tonnes and was almost twenty-three metres long. A total of six countries had been involved in its construction.

How long did Ellen's record breaking round-the-world voyage take?

Ellen circumnavigated the world in seventy-one days, fourteen hours, eighteen minutes and thirty-three seconds between November 2004 and February 2005.

What problems did she have to face during the voyage?

During the voyage, Ellen had to survive mountainous seas, high winds and floating icebergs. On one occasion the boat was in danger of being overturned by a large whale. In addition the generator broke down early on and there were always repairs to be carried out including climbing to the top of the mast.

What new award did she receive when she arrived safely back home?

Ellen became a Dame Commander of the British Empire. It was a special award given by the Queen that meant she could now be called Dame Ellen MacArthur. Later Ellen attended a special ceremony called an investiture in London where the Queen presented her with a silver medal.

When was the round-the-world record broken again?

Ellen's record was broken in January 2008 when Francis Joyon again sailed around the world, this time clipping more than fourteen days off the time. Ellen went over to France to be one of the first people to congratulate him when he arrived back. As she said, ' Records are made to be broken.'

What does Ellen MacArthur do now?

Ellen is still involved in yachting from her base at Cowes in the Isle of Wight. She continues to run the Ellen MacArthur Trust. Recently she has said she will devote her time to environmental issues especially our use of energy resources.

Lesson Plan 1

Lone sailor

History objectives
- To find out who Ellen MacArthur is.
- To find out how she became famous.

Resources

- Pictures of yachts and sailing ships.
- Coloured pencils
- Activity sheet 1-3
- Generic sheets 1, 2 and 6-8

Starting points: whole class

Display in the classroom, pictures, photographs and posters etc showing yachts and sailing ships. Children should be encouraged to talk about their own experiences of seeing sailing ships of different kinds at harbour festivals and during visits to the coast etc. Look in some detail at the vessels on display.

- What basic shapes are they?
- How does the shape help movement through the water?
- How many masts do they have?
- Where is the mast(s) positioned?
- How many sails are there?
- What shapes are they?
- How do the sizes of the sails vary?
- How are the yachts steered?
- How do they change direction?
- How many crew-members are needed?

Ask children if they can recall the names of any famous sailors from the past both from Britain and other countries. Names that might occur could include Leif Ericson, John Cabot, Francis Drake, Walter Raleigh, James Cook, Horatio Nelson, Ferdinand Magellan and Christopher Columbus. How long ago did they live? What famous voyages are they well known for?

Provide them also with details about more recent Britons who have been long distance sea travellers like Chay Blyth, Francis Chichester, Alec Rose, Clare Francis and Tracy Edwards. What yachts did they sail on? What journeys did they undertake? What records did they break?

Tell children they are going to find out more about another famous British sailor, Ellen MacArthur, who broke the record for sailing round the world single-handed in 2004-2005. Show them pictures/photographs of Ellen MacArthur and her sailing boat B&Q as shown on Generic sheet 1.

Use the timeline on Generic sheet 2 and the questions and answers on Generic sheet 6-8 to fill in more of the details about the life of Ellen MacArthur and how a series of major sailing achievements during the last fifteen years have made her famous. Highlight particular events like the round Britain solo sail (1995), the Vendee Globe (2002), the Route du Rhum (2003) and the round-the-world record-breaking voyage (2004-2005).

Group activities

Activity sheet 1
On this activity sheet, for children who need support with their literacy work, six statements are given about the life and achievements of Ellen MacArthur. Children are required to pick and circle with a coloured pencil the statements that are true. In addition, at the bottom of the sheet, they have to correct the statements that are not true. If extra tasks are needed, children could also be asked to write their own short true statements about Ellen MacArthur. These could be written on the back of the sheet.

Activity sheet 2
These children have to complete the sentences that have been written about the life and achievements of Ellen MacArthur. Six sentences are given and the correct words have to be chosen from the word bank given at the bottom of the sheet. Again, children should add extra detail about Ellen MacArthur on the back of the sheet. They could make up similar sentences with missing words and ask a friend to fill in the gaps.

Activity sheet 3
More able children are also provided with sentences about the life and achievements of Ellen MacArthur but this time they must provide their own endings. Help them with research if some answers are a little unclear. The question and answer section on Generic sheets 5-7 should be particularly useful. Children could work in pairs to exchange ideas before arriving at the most suitable endings for each of the six sentences. Then they have to write other information about Ellen MacArthur.

Plenary session

Revise the content of the lesson with a role-play session in which you play the part of Ellen MacArthur. Respond to children's questions by trying to provide some of the reasoning behind the decisions and the actions made by the famous sailor. Questions might include the following:

- Where were you born?
- What things were you interested in as a child?
- How did you first become interested in sailing?
- Who taught you to sail?
- Did you find learning to sail difficult?
- What was your first boat like?
- What is the most difficult thing about sailing round the world?
- What is the most enjoyable thing about sailing round the world?

Ideas for support

Preparation work will need to be done with all groups on sentence construction to make sure they are grammatically correct and contain the right punctuation. Keep sentences concise and relevant and avoid over elaboration.

When children are writing their own sentences, encourage them to pick information and incidents that are central to Ellen MacArthur's life and achievements.

Provide word lists and word banks where necessary especially when children are using the names of boats, locations and events e.g. Iduna, Le Poisson, Southern Ocean, Martinique, Route du Rhum and Vendee Globe.

Ideas for extension

Ask children to choose one of the famous sailors from the past, perhaps one of those listed in the lesson notes e.g. Ericson, Cook, Cabot, Magellan, Nelson. They should avoid Sir Francis Drake as this point as he will feature in more detail in one of the later lessons.

They should find out more about the chosen sailor's most important voyages and the routes they followed, how they financed their excursions, what important contributions they made during the 'age of discovery' and what famous ships they were associated with.

If small groups of children work on different subjects they can present their findings, once completed, to the rest of the class giving much greater coverage overall.

Lone sailor

Name ....

Circle with a coloured pencil the sentences about Ellen MacArthur that are true.

Write correct versions of the incorrect sentences at the bottom of the page.

Ellen MacArthur was born in London.

Her aunt first got her interested in sailing.

Ellen's first sailing boat was called Two Shillings.

Ellen sailed around the coast of Britain in a boat called Iduna.

The Route du Rhum is a sailing race across the Atlantic Ocean.

The round-the-world voyage in B&Q took Ellen three months.

Lone sailor

Activity Sheet 2

Name ....

Complete the following sentences about Ellen MacArthur. Use the word bank at the bottom of the sheet to help you.

Ellen saved up all her spare _____ to buy her first boat.

Ellen had her first sailing lesson when she was _____ years-old.

Le Poisson was the name of the boat that Ellen bought in _____

The Route du Rhum is a sailing _____ across the Atlantic Ocean.

Floating _____ were a danger on the round the world record breaking voyage.

The round the world record breaking voyage took Ellen just over ten _____

Write other things you know about Ellen MacArthur below.

_____
_____
_____
_____
_____
_____
_____
_____

Word bank
icebergs   race   France   ten   money   weeks

CURRICULUM FOCUS • Famous journeys 97

Activity Sheet 3

Lone sailor

Name ....

Complete the following sentences about Ellen MacArthur.

Ellen went sailing with her aunt when _____

Ellen got the money to buy her first boat by _____

In 1995, Ellen sailed her boat Iduna _____

In the Vendee Globe event, Ellen _____

Some of the dangers Ellen faced on her round the world voyage were _____

_____

The round the world voyage took Ellen _____

What else do you know about Ellen MacArthur? Write your own sentences here.

_____
_____
_____
_____
_____
_____
_____
_____

98 CURRICULUM FOCUS • Famous journeys

Round the world

LESSON 2 PLAN

History objectives
- To discuss the qualities needed to be a solitary round-the-world sailor.
- To compare the important similarities and differences between the round-the-world voyages of Sir Francis Drake and Dame Ellen MacArthur.

Resources

- World maps and charts
- Coloured pencils
- Portraits of Sir Francis Drake
- Diagrams/pictures of Elizabethan sailing ships
- Activity sheets 1-3
- Generic sheets 1, 3 and 4

Starting points: whole class

Talk about Ellen MacArthur as an individual. What can we find out about her from incidents in her life and from the quotes that are featured on Generic sheet 4?

- Which quotes are most revealing?
- Which ones seem to sum her up best?

Ask children to list what they think are the type of qualities needed to carry out a solo round-the-world voyage? Think about qualities like physical strength, sailing skills, self-confidence, perseverance, determination, resilience etc. What evidence is there that Ellen MacArthur possessed these qualities?

Can children think of incidences in their own lives when they have needed to show some of these qualities? In what situations did they have to use them? Would they have the qualities needed to carry out a long solo sea voyage?

On a large world map or on the whiteboard, show children the route followed by Ellen MacArthur on her round-the-world voyage, 2004-2005. Use arrows on the route to indicate the directions in which she sailed. Point out the major oceans she sailed through during the voyage i.e. Atlantic Ocean, Southern Ocean, Indian Ocean and the Pacific Ocean. Show also important lines of latitude that she crossed like the Equator, the Tropic of Cancer and the Tropic of Capricorn.

Also show, in order to make comparisons, the route followed in the sixteenth century by Sir Francis Drake, who between 1577 and 1580, became the first British sailor to circumnavigate the world. Drake sailed first to West Africa and then crossed the Atlantic to reach Brazil in South America. He continued round the tip of South America before heading north along its western coastline. Drake continued along the coastline of Central America and North America (as far as the present site of Vancouver) before heading out into the Pacific. He sailed as far as Indonesia, crossed the Indian Ocean and rounded the Cape of Good Hope before returning home via the Atlantic.

Take the opportunity to find out more about Drake's story.

- Where did he come from?
- How did he learn his sailing skills?
- Why did Tudor sailors like Drake find exploration so important?
- What were his motives for going round the world?
- Was it for greater personal wealth and possessions?
- Was it for the general benefit of the country?

Then look at the main similarities and differences between the voyages made by Francis Drake and Ellen MacArthur. Some of the main points for discussion are given below. **Note:** EM is used as an abbreviation for Ellen MacArthur and FD for Francis Drake.

Similarities

- Both EM and FD succeeded in their goal and circumnavigated the globe by sail.
- The reigning monarch rewarded both sailors on their return. FD was knighted by Queen Elizabeth I on board his ship The Golden Hind. EM was made a Dame Commander of the British Empire by Queen Elizabeth II at an investiture at Buckingham Palace.

Differences

- EM took just over ten weeks to complete the voyage while FD was away for almost three years.
- Both sailors took different routes. EM sailed south and then headed east to round the tip of Africa while FD, after sailing south, turned west towards South America. EM covered about 50600 km while FD travelled almost 58000 km.
- EM was always racing against time to beat the record and did the journey non-stop. FD stopped in a number of places to pick up food and also to carry out repairs.
- EM carried out the round-the-world trip entirely on her own. FD started his expedition with five ships and a total of about two hundred men. He returned with only one ship, The Golden Hind, and about sixty surviving crew-

members. He always had colleagues to consult and crew-members to sail the ship for him.
- EM's yacht B&Q was purpose built to complete the voyage, twenty-three metres long and weighing about eight tonnes. FD's Golden Hind weighed about 300 tonnes and was thirty-seven metres long. FD had to plot his course using largely the Sun, the Moon and the stars. EM had all the latest technology including satellite navigation.
- EM was able to keep in touch with her headquarters throughout the voyage speaking on the telephone and sending e-mails and photographs. Other sailors brought home some news of FD but it was not until he arrived back home that people knew where he had been and what he had achieved.

Activity sheet 1
The world map on this sheet for less able children shows the routes followed by both Francis Drake and Ellen MacArthur on their round-the-world voyages. Children are required firstly to label the four main world oceans. A word bank is provided to help them with spelling. They are also required to place arrows on the two routes using a coloured pencil to show the directions followed by both of the sailors. After both sailing to the south, Ellen turned to the east while Drake steered west to travel from West Africa to South America.

Activity sheet 2
The same world map is also shown on this activity sheet with the routes of the two round-the-world sailors marked. Children need to label the main oceans, Atlantic, Pacific, Southern and Indian, as well as the Tropic of Cancer, the Equator, the Tropic of Capricorn and the main continents. They will need to do their own research on the large world map to find these locations. Again, a coloured pencil should be used to put arrows on the map showing the contrasting directions travelled by the two sailors.

Activity sheet 3
For more able children, the same map is provided but this time only the route followed by Sir Francis Drake is shown. Children should firstly label the four main oceans, the Equator and the two Tropics and the major continents. They should then use a coloured pencil to mark on the course steered by Ellen MacArthur. Arrows should be added to both routes to show direction. Following the activity, split the group into pairs and ask them to discuss the major differences in the routes taken by the two sailors.

Plenary session

Recap on the discussion held with children at the beginning of the lesson about the qualities needed by a single-handed round the world sailor. Is everyone capable of completing such a voyage or does it require a very special person?

Display a large world map on the whiteboard and ask for volunteers to come out and show the routes followed by both Sir Francis Drake and Dame Ellen MacArthur on their round-the-world voyages.

Ask some members who completed Activity sheet 3 to report on the major differences in the routes taken by the two sailors and in what ways the two journeys differed.

Ideas for support

Children need to be conversant with a world map in order to follow the routes carefully. They should be familiar with the continents, the major oceans and important lines of latitude like the equator and the two tropics. Knowledge of the main points of compass direction should also be sound so children can successfully use arrows to mark on routes. Similarity and difference is an important historical concept, so spend time reinforcing comparisons between the two sailors and their motivation, the times in which they sailed on their journeys, the vessels they used, the aids they had to help them etc.

Ideas for extension

Talk about the navigational difficulties faced by sailors in Tudor times. How did seafarers find their way? There were no precise instruments and unreliable charts and maps. Those drawn at the time prove sailors did not know the exact shape and size of some lands and that others, like Australia and New Zealand, were missing completely.
Find out what life was like at sea for Tudor sailors. Ordinary seamen were often 'pressed' or coerced into taking long, dangerous voyages. Crews spent most of their time feeling cold and wet and wondering if they would ever see their homes and families again. Find out about the daily routine of sailors. What did they have to eat? What illnesses and diseases did they face? What punishments could they expect if they did not obey orders?

Round the world

Name ....

The map below shows the round the world voyages made by Sir Francis Drake (1577-1580) and Dame Ellen MacArthur (2004-2005).

Label the main oceans on the world map. A word bank is provided to help you.

Mark arrows on the map to show the directions in which the two sailors travelled.

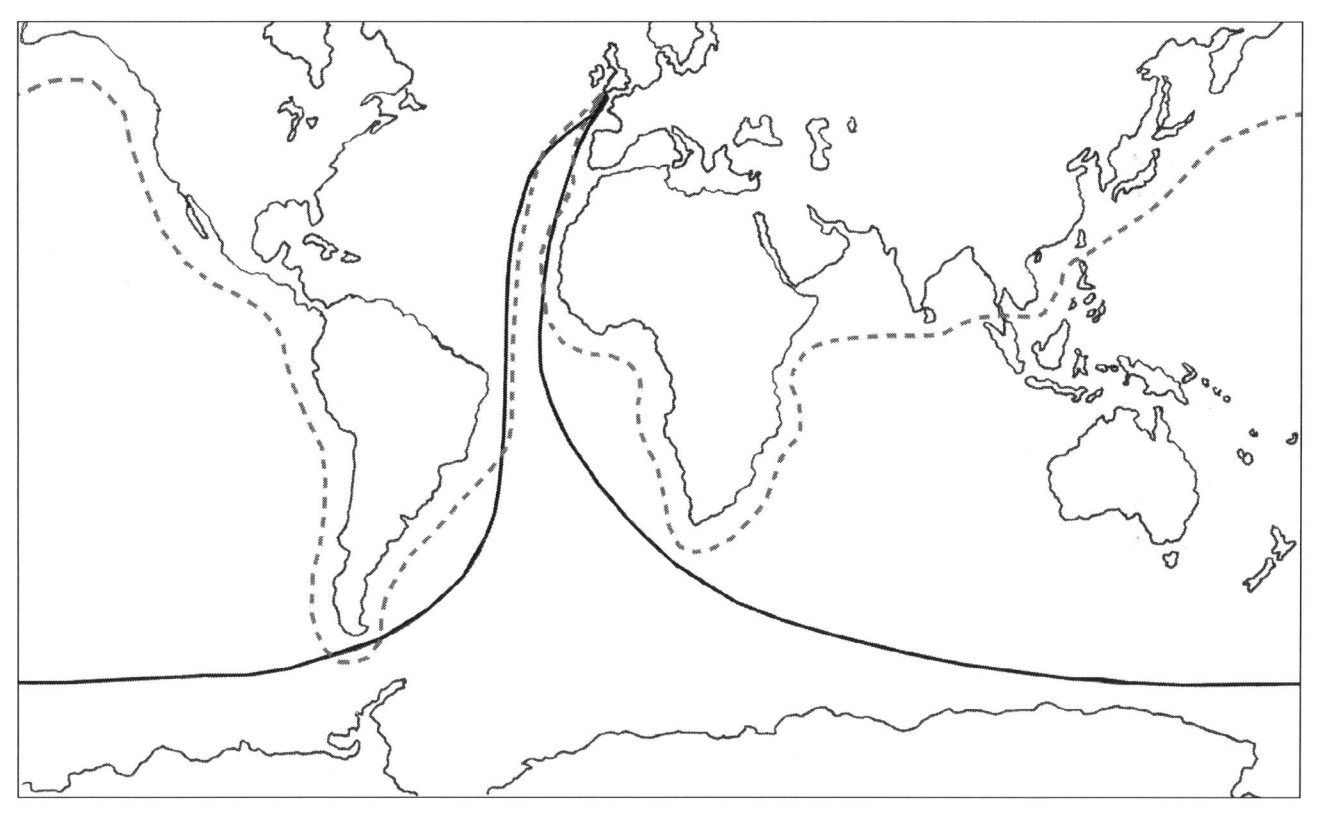

———— Dame Ellen MacArthur

— — — Sir Francis Drake

Word bank
Atlantic Ocean   Pacific Ocean   Indian Ocean   Southern Ocean

CURRICULUM FOCUS • Famous journeys **101**

Round the world

Name ....

The map below shows the round the world voyages made by Sir Francis Drake (1577-1580) and Dame Ellen MacArthur (2004-2005).

Label the main oceans of the world on the map, the Equator, The Tropic of Cancer and The Tropic of Capricorn and the main continents, Africa, Asia, America, Europe, Australasia and Antarctica.

Mark arrows on the map to show the directions in which the two sailors travelled.

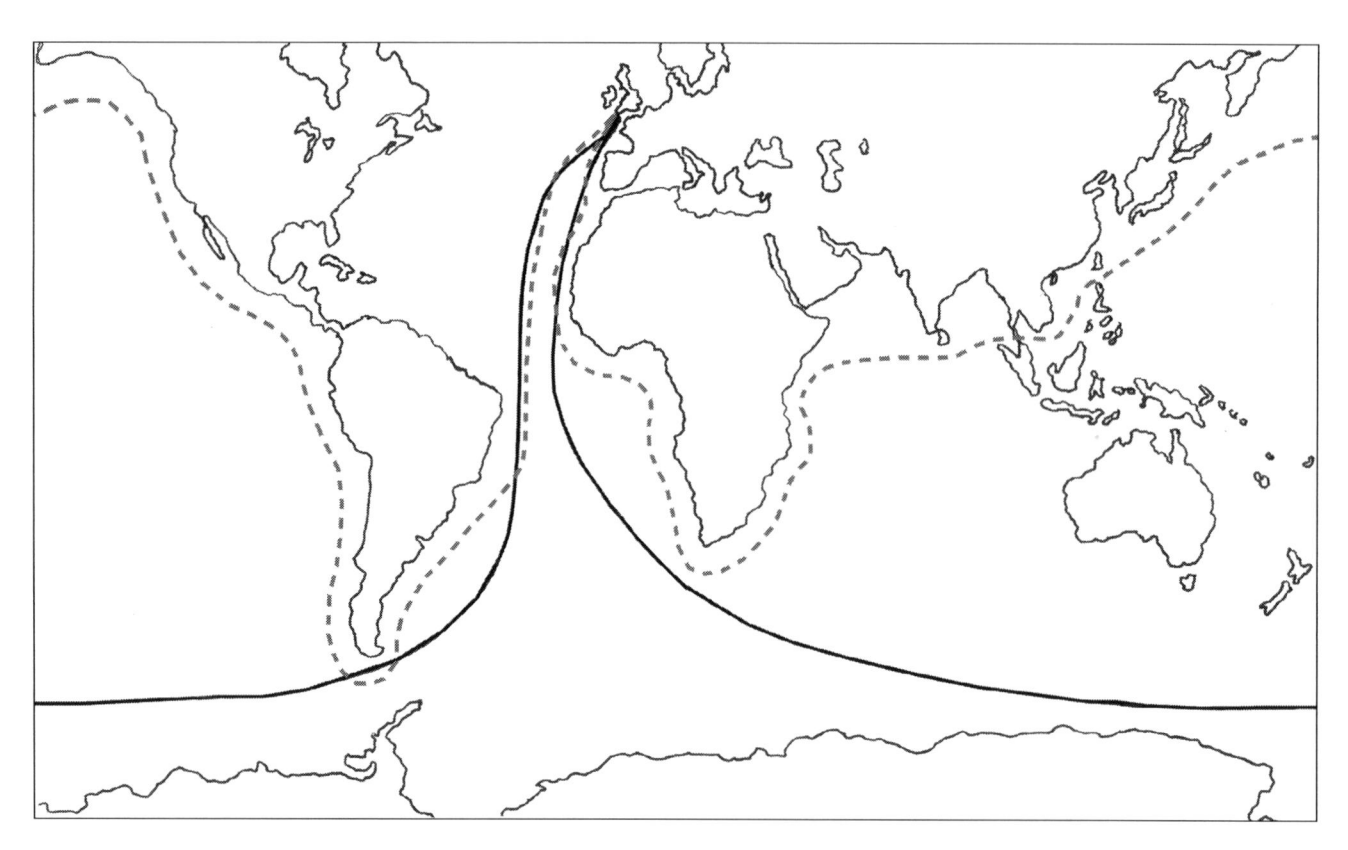

─────── Dame Ellen MacArthur

─ ─ ─ Sir Francis Drake

102 CURRICULUM FOCUS · Famous journeys

Round the world

Activity Sheet 3

Name _____

The map below shows the round the world voyage made by Sir Francis Drake (1577-1580).

Label the main oceans, the main continents, the Equator and the Tropics of Cancer and Capricorn.

Carefully add to the map the round the world route sailed by Dame Ellen MacArthur (2004-2005) and put arrows on both routes to show in which directions the two sailors travelled.

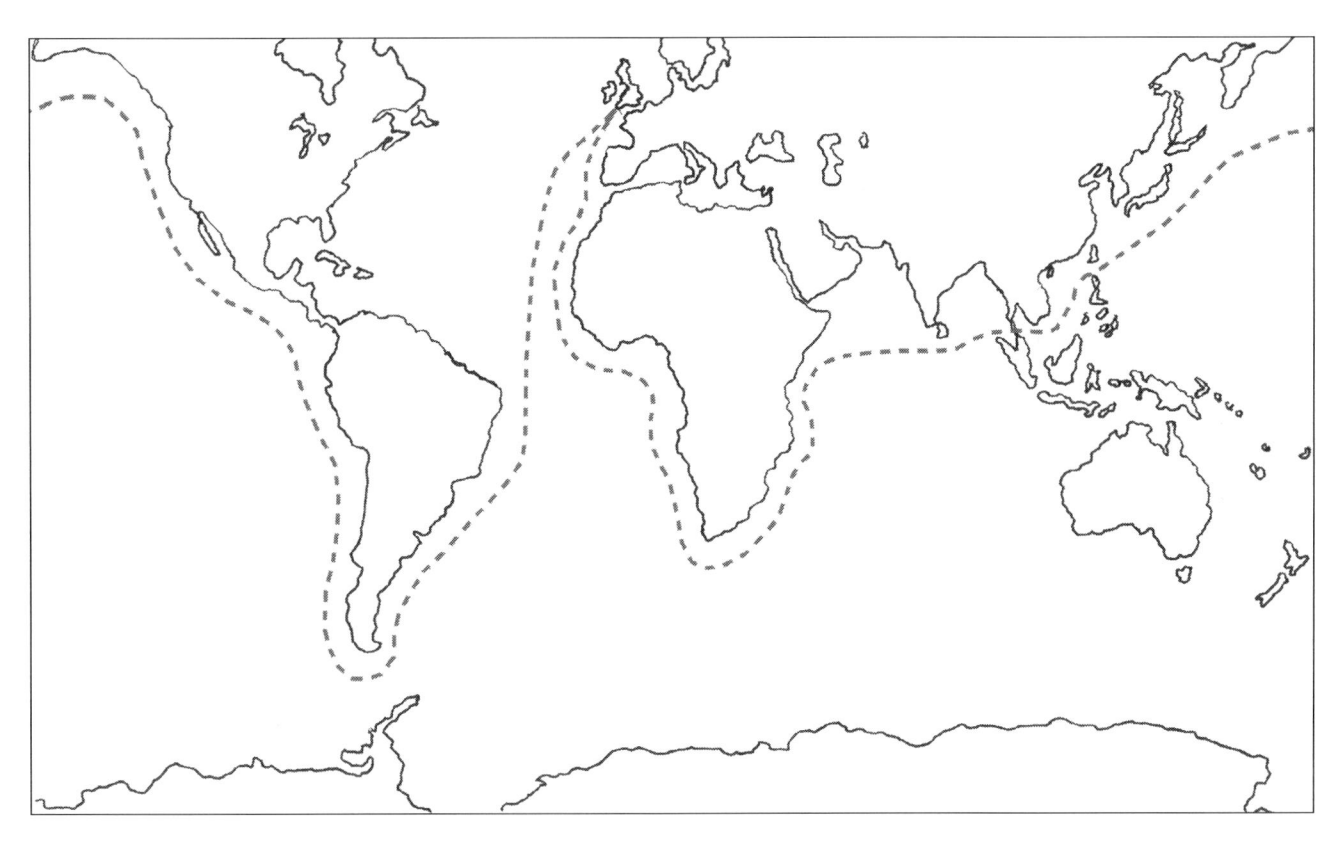

– – – Sir Francis Drake

CURRICULUM FOCUS • Famous journeys **103**

LESSON PLAN 3

All at sea

History objectives
- To investigate the basic principles of sailing boat design.
- To compare and contrast the development of sailing vessels throughout history.

Resources

- Pictures of ships, boats and watercraft
- Large sheets of paper, pencils
- Offcuts of balsa and thin wood
- Saws, sandpaper
- Small plastic bottles
- Paper, card, thin fabric
- Scissors, glue, sticky tape
- Dowel rods, kebab sticks, plant sticks
- Water tank made from plastic drainpipe
- Hair drier
- Pastels, crayons, paints
- Elastic bands
- Propellers, paddles
- Generic sheets 1 and 5
- Activity sheets 1-3

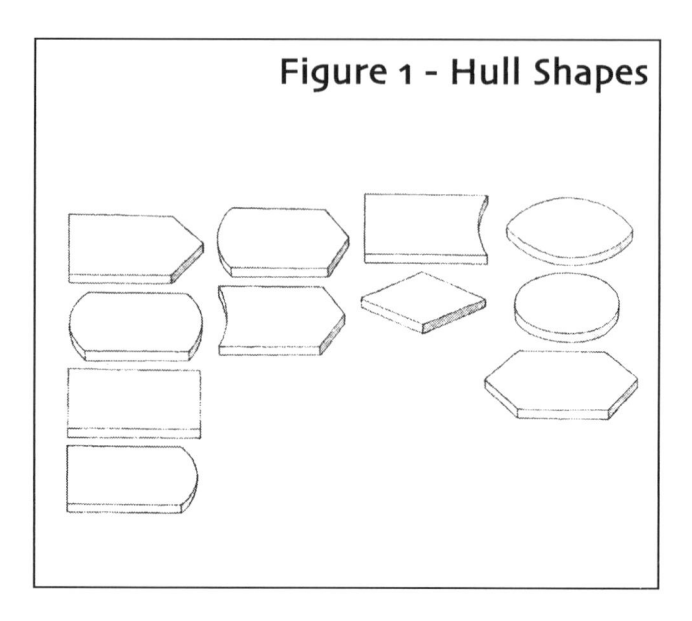

Before the history lesson

Involve children in practical design and technology tasks that will help them gain a greater insight into the basic principles involved in sailing boat designing and building.

One of the major questions facing boat designers and constructors of ocean going yachts and sailing boats is how these large objects will float and move through the water under wind power.

Use a range of different reference materials to gather together a collection of pictures of ships and boats and other watercraft showing a range of hull shapes. It may also be possible to stimulate further observation and discussion by mounting a display of model boats in the classroom.

Hull shapes

Divide the class into small groups of three or four. Provide each group with a large sheet of paper and pencils and encourage them to design three or four different hull shapes which are approximately the same size but have different features. See Figure 1. Once the children are happy with their designs, use tracing paper to transfer the designs to balsa or other types of thin wood. With adult help and supervision, the shapes should be cut out carefully with a saw and any rough edges smoothed with sandpaper. When the models are ready they should be placed in a suitable water tank. Gentle hand propulsion should then be used to see how well they move and how buoyant they are. Extend the activity by asking children to construct boats with more built-up hull shapes. Consider improving the stability by splitting the hull into two parts like a catamaran or try making the hulls from plastic bottles to see if they are more stable than the ones made from other materials. See Figure 2.

Figure 1 - Hull Shapes

Figure 2 - Multi-hulls

Catamaran

Trimaran

104 CURRICULUM FOCUS • Famous journeys

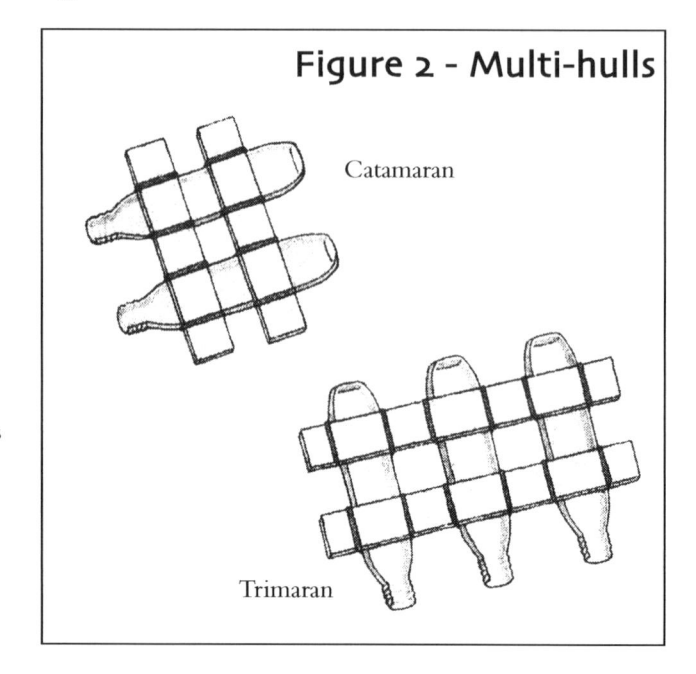

Figure 3 - Sail Shapes

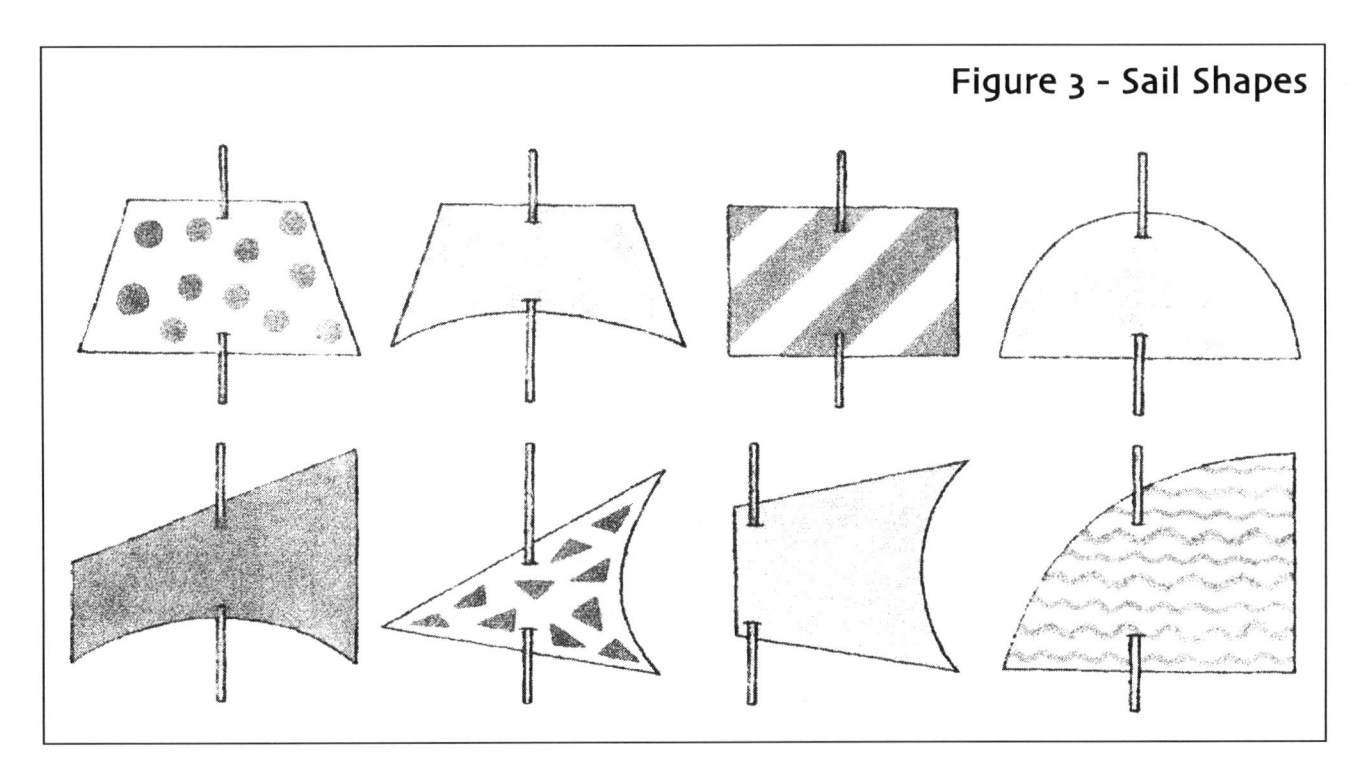

Under sail

Add some sails to the model boats to propel them through the water. Try a variety of different sail shapes to see which is the most effective. See Figure 3. Experiment with different kinds of paper, card, plastic sheets etc and also try a range of different thin fabrics. Attach sails to masts fashioned from thin dowel rods or kebab sticks. They should then be secured into the hull shapes already made.

To test these boats, a long thin water tank is best. Use a section of plastic drainpipe about two to three metres long and mount it on wooden blocks to make it stable. This will provide a narrow channel that helps keep the prototype boats moving along a straight course. An electric hair drier should provide the required amount of wind. See Figure 4.

Develop the construction tasks further by experimenting with methods of waterproofing the boat-building materials. Try coverings like pastel crayon, wax crayon and oil and water-based paints. Which works best? Or consider other methods of propulsion apart from wind power. Ask children to experiment with elastic bands, for example, to work some form of propeller or paddle system at the rear of the boat that can be used to drive it forwards. Figure 5.

Starting points: whole class

After the children have completed various models in the design and technology lessons, talk about how sailing ships have developed over time.

Start by looking at the three sailing vessels shown on Generic sheet 5, the Viking longship, Drake's The Golden Hind and Brunel's first large ocean going ship, the PSS Great Western. Talk about how the design of these ships have changed sail power at sea. Provide children with some background information about each one.

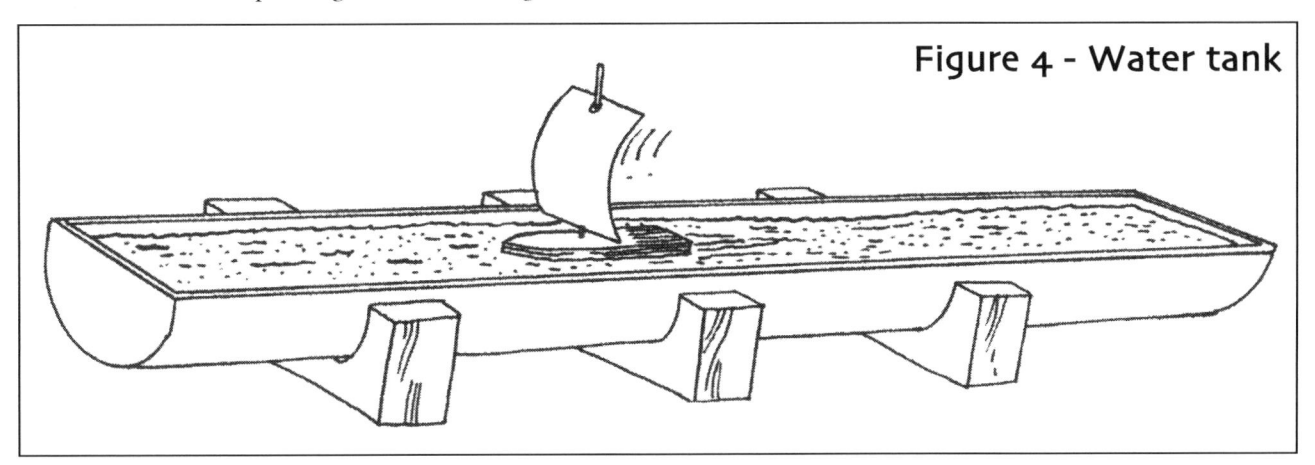

Figure 4 - Water tank

Figure 5 - Powered boats

Propeller driven — Elastic band

Paddle driven — Elastic band

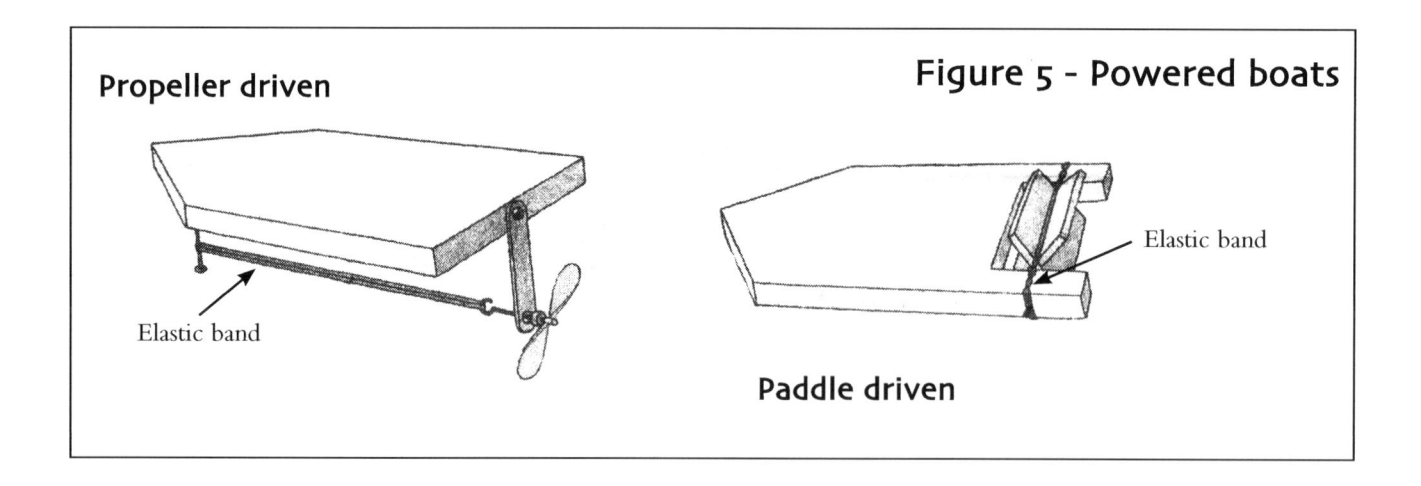

Viking longship

We know about the basic dimensions of Viking longships from several that have been excavated in Scandinavia. They were usually about 25m long and 5m wide. The height of the mast was about 10m. The mast carried a single fabric sail and oars were used when there was no wind or the vessel was in shallow water. A rudder at the stern steered the vessel and benches that the crew sat on doubled as storage chests. There were usually no more than about 30 men aboard.

The Golden Hind

The Golden Hind, originally called The Pelican, was about 38m long and 8m wide. It had three masts and five decks. There were square sails and one lateen-a triangular sail at the front of the vessel set on a long yard at a forty-five degree angle to the mast. It could carry a crew of about eighty but there was usually less. It was well armed and would usually carry about twenty cannon guns.

PSS Great Western

The Paddle Steamship Great Western, 76m long and 18m wide, was launched in Bristol in 1837. It was equipped with both paddles and sails and was designed to carry 150 passengers. It took the vessel about two weeks to cross the Atlantic, a route that it worked for about eight years. The wooden-built ship was a side-wheel paddle steamer with four masts to carry auxiliary sails. They not only provided extra power but were used in rough seas to keep the ship on an even keel and both paddles in the water. After being used as a troopship during the Crimean War, the PSS Great Western was broken up.

Compare these vessels with Ellen MacArthur's B&Q yacht. (Details about this yacht are given in the Teachers' Notes.)

- How does each sailing ship best suit the purpose for which they were intended?
- Which of the vessels discussed would children prefer to make a long sea voyage in? Ask them to give reasons for their choice.

Group activities

Activity sheet 1
This activity sheet requires children to place the correct labels on each sailing vessel. Mount each of the pictures on card, cut out the labels and stick them carefully underneath. They should also be able to order the vessels correctly on a timeline.

Activity sheet 2
Here the children not only have to label the ships they are also required to write a sentence about each one mentioning what they consider to be each vessel's most important feature. A word bank is provided to help with spelling. Again, ensure children can arrange the vessels in time order.

Activity sheet 3
More able children should arrange the labels under the correct pictures and then place them correctly on a timeline. They also have to write about the type of sailing ship they would prefer to travel on and to explain why.

Plenary session

Share findings from the practical design and technology sessions and discuss the results carried out on the model boats.

- Which hull shapes proved to be the most successful?
- Which shaped sail caught the wind best?
- Which type of fabric/material made the best sail?
- What was the best way of securing the sail to the mast?
- Which was the best method of waterproofing the hull of a model boat?
- Were models more stable when multi-hulls (catamarans, trimarans) were used?
- Did other materials, e.g. plastic, float better than wood?

- Can children now identify some of the main principles involved in designing and constructing a successful sailing boat?

Recap on the comparisons made between the four sailing vessels.

- What are the similarities between the four vessels investigated?
- What are their major differences?
- How have the reasons for using sailing vessels changed over the years?
- Why has wind power remained popular as a way of travelling by sea?

Ideas for support

Some children will need support with the measuring, cutting, fixing and testing aspects of the boat-building activities. It may be necessary to have some materials already prepared for the children to work with.

Safety note:

It is essential that all teachers, support staff and helpers involved in practical activities are fully conversant with the school and local authority rules that apply to these areas of the curriculum and ensure that they are always carried out.

Ideas for extension

Find out more about the sailing ships and individuals featured during the lesson. How far did Viking ships travel on their expeditions of discovery? Look particularly at the career of Leif Ericson. What did Sir Francis Drake do following his return from the circumnavigation of the world? What role did Drake play in the defeat of the Spanish Armada? How was the PSS Great Western used commercially following her trans-Atlantic voyages? What was her final fate?

Ask someone who belongs to a local sailing club to come into school and talk to the children about the activities they carry out. Where do they sail? What sort of sailing boats do they use? Do they run courses for young people to learn how to sail?

Watch the media for news of international sailing events that are being held like the America's Cup and the Vendee Globe. What sailing events will be included in the 2012 Olympic Games when it is held in this country? Where will these sailing events be held?

ACTIVITY SHEET 1

All at sea

Name ....

Cut out the pictures of sailing ships and match them with the correct label.

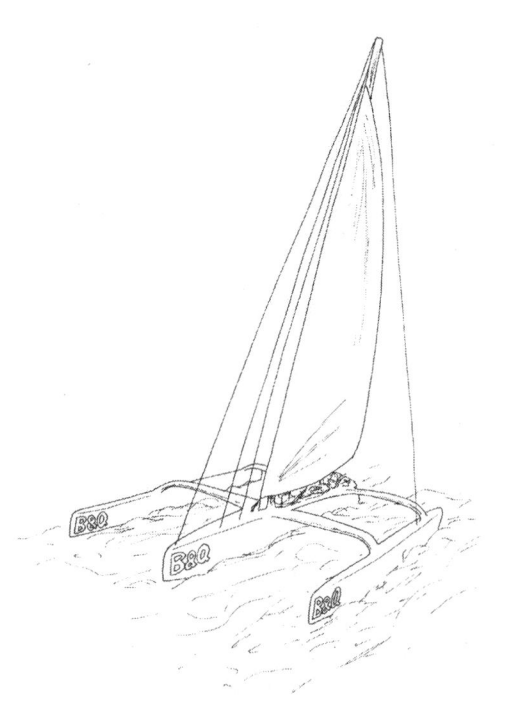

| Viking longship | The Golden Hind | B&Q yacht | PSS Great Western |

Place the sailing ships in the correct order on a timeline.

108 CURRICULUM FOCUS • Famous journeys

All at sea

Name ....

2 ACTIVITY SHEET

Cut out the pictures of the sailing ships and match them with the correct label.

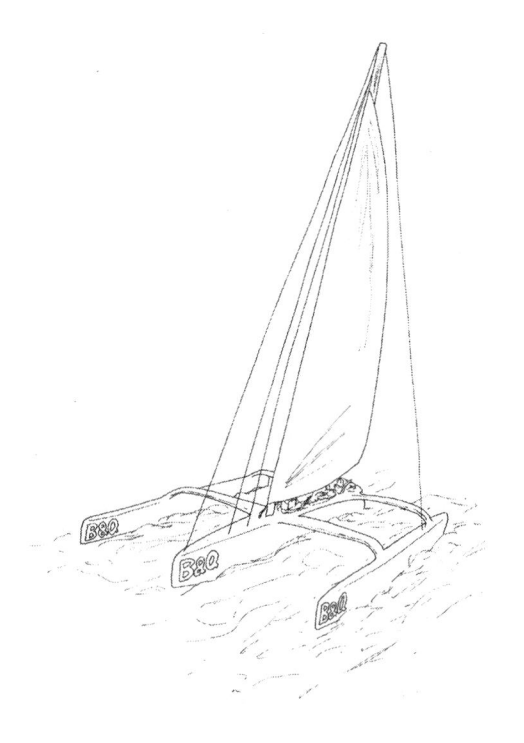

| Viking longship | The Golden Hind | B&Q yacht | PSS Great Western |

Place the sailing ships in the correct order on a timeline.

Write a sentence about each one to explain why they proved to be effective sailing ships.

CURRICULUM FOCUS • Famous journeys 109

ACTIVITY SHEET 3

All at sea

Name ....

Cut out the pictures of the sailing ships and match them with the correct label.

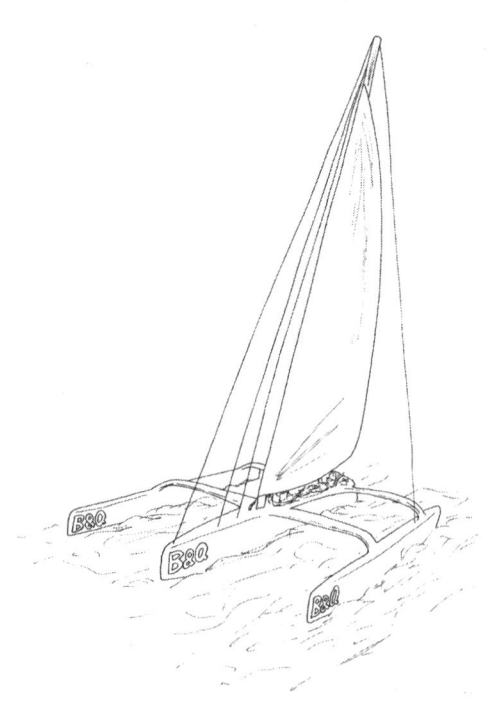

| Viking longship | The Golden Hind | B&Q yacht | PSS Great Western |

Place the sailing ships in the correct order on a timeline.

Write a short paragraph about each vessel explaining why they were such effective sailing ships.

Which one would you prefer to make a long sea voyage in? Give your reasons.

CURRICULUM FOCUS • Famous journeys

Useful resources:

Amelia Earhart

www.ameliaearhart.com
www.ameliaearhartmuseum.org (Atchison, Kansas)
www.acepilots.com/earhart

Books written by Amelia Earhart
20 hours, 40 minutes (1928)

The Fun of It (1932)

Last Flight (1937)

Films
Flight of Freedom (1943)

Amelia Earhart (TV version 1976)

Amelia Earhart: The Final Flight (1994)

Amelia (2009)

Roald Amundsen:

www.coolantarctica.com
www.cybersleuth-kids.com
www.south-pole.com

Books by Amundsen
An Account of the Norwegian Antarctic Expedition in the Fram 1910-1912 (1912)

Our Polar Flight: The Amundsen-Ellsworth Polar Flight (1925)

My Life as an Explorer (1927)

Films and TV
The Last Place on Earth, TV series based on the book Scott and Amundsen by Robert Huntford.

The Red Tent (film starring Sean Connery)
Roald Amundsen appears as a great explorer in the 2008 strategy video game Civilisation Revolution.

Neil Armstrong:

www.nasa.gov/worldbook/armstrong_neil_worldbook

youtube.com video of Moon landing
video.google.com interview with Neil Armstrong

The Life of Neil A Armstrong by James R Hansen (2005) official biography

Use websites of NASA's Mission Control Center at Houston, Texas, the Space Shuttle Project and Kennedy Space Center, Florida.

Ellen MacArthur

www.ellenmacarthur.com
www.ellenmacarthurcancertrust.org
www.ellenmacarthurfoundation.org

Books written by Ellen MacArthur
Taking on the World (autobiography)

Full Circle and Race Against Time (dealing with round the world record breaking voyage)

Notes

Notes